HACK Your Journal

STAY ORGANIZED & RECORD

Everything that Matters

WITH ONE NOTEBOOK

LARK
New York

LARK
New York

An Imprint of Sterling Publishing Co., Inc.
1166 Avenue of the Americas
New York, NY 10036

ISBN 978-1-4547-1068-4

Distributed in Canada by Sterling Publishing Co., Inc.
c/o Canadian Manda Group, 664 Annette Street
Toronto, Ontario M6S 2C8, Canada
Distributed in the United Kingdom by GMC Distribution Services
Castle Place, 166 High Street, Lewes, East Sussex BN7 1XU, England
Distributed in Australia by NewSouth Books
45 Beach Street, Coogee, NSW 2034, Australia

For information about custom editions, special sales, and premium and corporate purchases,
please contact Sterling Special Sales at 800-805-5489 or specialsales@sterlingpublishing.com.

Manufactured in Canada

2 4 6 8 10 9 7 5 3 1

sterlingpublishing.com
larkcrafts.com

Interior design by Christine Heun
Cover design by Elizabeth Mihaltse Lindy
Interior and cover photography by Chris Bain

Photo Credits
iStock: ©artisteer: 6, 54; ©DNY59: 28, 60, 135 (eraser); ©mbongorus: 23 (clip)

CONTENTS

INTRODUCTION

Since they've existed, journals have always done double duty. Their pages have been homes for diary entries full of thoughts and reflections. They've been used for record-keeping and note-taking.

Today, the journal wears even more hats. There are now journaling setups that turn a notebook into a one-stop shop for organizing, recording, tracking, and reflecting. These hybrid journals have become tools that help you build healthy habits on one page, plan a vacation on the next, and organize your busy Saturday on the following spread. They now combine the functions of a diary, planner, and organizer and have quickly become the best way to tackle everything from meal planning to scheduling household chores. Some journalers have even turned their notebooks into an artistic outlet, designing pages that are as useful and practical as they are creative.

If you've seen these journals and wondered how you can do so much with just a simple notebook, this book is here to help. It'll explain the advantages of journaling, teach you how to set up your journal, outline the essential tools,

and best of all, provide lots of ideas for page layouts designed by seven journalers. The layouts are split into different categories based on their function, and they showcase a wide range of styles and all you can do with just a pen and paper. Step-by-step instructions will make the designs approachable.

Each page layout is also customizable and can be easily adapted to any personal preference or journaling method that you're already using. You can decorate the pages however you like, skip any extra features that you might not have time to include, add color to black-and-white spreads, and even pick and choose elements of individual layouts to create one that perfectly suits your needs. Practice pages in the back of the book give you space to experiment and try out some of the designs.

Whether you are completely new to journaling and want to find a way to make your planning more efficient or a seasoned journaler looking for a fresh ideas, you'll find an endless amount of inspiration and tons of practical tips to turn your notebook into an essential tool for staying organized.

Getting Started

There are countless ways to keep a journal, but in this book, we'll be using the term *journaling* to refer specifically to any type of journaling that lets you write down in one place anything and everything you need to record, track, and remember. There's no need to divide your journal into sections ahead of time. Gone are the days of juggling a separate diary, planner, or random scraps of paper filled with lists and reminders! Your journal becomes the place for anything you want to write down, whether they're calendars listing your upcoming appointments, diary entries, meeting notes, or ideas for your next art project.

On each page, you'll create page layouts where you can design your own planning pages, write customized to-do lists, and track important information about your routines. In this book, the terms *page layout* (or *layout*) and *spread* refer to any pages with a design. You'll add each layout as you go along; there's no need to think of an overarching hierarchy or specific sections before you get started.

If this already has your head spinning, don't worry—we'll break down how it works in practice soon. Just remember that all we're doing here is using your journal as a catchall for everything that you want to write down.

WHY JOURNAL?

Building your own journal from scratch might look like a daunting and complex undertaking, but there are many important advantages to using a customizable journaling method that you might not find with other planning and organizational tools.

One of the most important elements of a journaling method like this is that it is flexible and adaptable. While there are many digital planning tools available, an electronic calendar or a smartphone app doesn't have the versatility of a blank notebook, where each page can be adapted for any purpose. Unlike a preprinted planner, which has already decided how any information you record will be organized, a journal gives you the freedom to write things down as you go along and use as much or as little space as you need at that exact moment. Your journal will grow organically without any need to spend extra time dividing it into sections before you get started. You won't run out of space or have any extra pages or unused sections that you've skipped because they weren't what you looking for. Plus, because you know your own organizational needs better than a preprinted planner, you can design each page exactly how you want.

Making your own page layouts not only puts you in charge, it also gives you a moment to check in with yourself. Because anything you write on the page is entirely up to you, the very act of putting together a spread lets you take a quick break from your busy day, think about how you've been spending your time, and reflect on the things that have already happened and the things that have yet to come. Through journaling, you'll find space on the page and off the page to slow down and take some time for yourself.

Creating a layout from scratch or taking time to put together a to-do list every day might sound like the last thing you want to do, especially if your schedule is bursting at the seams, but journaling will ultimately help you save time. By keeping everything that matters to you in one central location and taking the time to stay organized, you'll ultimately use your time more efficiently and save yourself the worry of accidentally forgetting or missing something important.

HOW TO STAY MOTIVATED:
TIPS FOR MAKING JOURNALING A DAILY HABIT

BY CRISTINA TAMAS

Throughout all the years that I've been journaling, I've come to realize that it's a trial-and-error process. Finding a method that works for me, one I am able to adapt to any situation easily. This, has helped me make journaling a daily habit. I'll share the most important tips that I've learned throughout my journey.

Try not to let inspiration overwhelm you. There's nothing worse than beginning something and feeling overwhelmed right from the get-go. It defeats the whole purpose, right? But if you're anything like me, you probably also feel like you can't start something until you've learned all about it and gathered all the inspiration that you could get, whether it's from a social media site or an online video. While this is a great thing to do at the beginning because it gets your creative juices flowing, be mindful that too much inspiration can have the opposite effect—it can become overwhelming, make you set high expectations for your journal, and become afraid of failure. Instead of comparing your journal to others and putting pressure on yourself, try to understand that you will be on your own journey.

* **Start off simple.** Begin journaling with basic layouts (e.g. spreads for planning by month, week, or day) and add more types of pages as you go along. While you're looking for inspiration, make a list of all the spreads and pages that you think might help you organize your life. Create pages for the more approachable ideas first, and make sure your journal doesn't become too high-maintenance for your lifestyle. Once you find layouts that work, you'll be able to start experimenting with other spreads without becoming overwhelmed or discouraged.

* **Be patient with yourself**. Understand that finding a way of journaling that works for you is indeed a journey. As we go through life, our needs change and our journals have to adapt as well. Be patient and allow yourself to learn from mistakes. Perfectionism has its place but not in your journal!

* **Make it a part of your daily routine**. Creating a habit isn't always easy, and sometimes you need a little push. Set aside a few minutes every day for writing in your journal. You can always create reminders on your phone or leave notes on your desk to make sure you don't forget to include journaling into your daily routine.

* **Reevaluate your journaling method**. If you find that journaling has become a chore to you, try to take a step back and reevaluate what you're doing. Ask yourself why certain parts may or may not be important or relevant anymore. Determine what works and what doesn't, and understand that letting go of certain parts doesn't mean failure. On the contrary, it shows progress with finding a more efficient journaling method that fits your needs. Don't be afraid to experiment with new ideas and to step out of your comfort zone—it's the only way to avoid getting stuck or losing motivation.

* **There are no rules to journaling**. Your journal is going to be as unique as you are, so there are absolutely no set rules that you should follow except your own. While daily journaling can help you tremendously in your personal development process, you don't necessarily have to use your journal every single day. There have been times where I've skipped entire pages because I lost my motivation or simply because my way of journaling wasn't working for me anymore. Other times, you simply need a break, and that's perfectly understandable—you can't pour from an empty cup. Whatever the case, it's always a good idea to just turn the page and continue where you left off.

* **Your journal can be anything—make it your own**. While I do wish my journal could also do the dishes for me, it truly does help me with almost every area of my life. I use it to write down my ideas, plan my day, record my feelings, draw in when I am bored or feeling creative, and even keep myself accountable for things that I want to improve in my life. Thus, my journal is my number one personal development tool. Whether you're a minimalist or a creative spirit, whether you have artistic abilities or not, your journal should serve as a tool to express yourself and help you grow as a person. Trust your own process and enjoy the journey!

SETTING UP YOUR JOURNAL

With the general concept of journaling under your belt, let's review some basic pages and features that will help you get started.

Here's a quick note to keep in mind before we dive in: the guidelines outlined in this section (and elsewhere) are just general suggestions. Your journal does not need to include all the pages listed here. Treat everything that you see in this book as a springboard for honing your own unique approach to journaling, rather than as strict rules that you have to follow. This is especially true for the specific page layouts that are featured later in the book, where each contributor has catered their designs to suit their personal needs. If your version of a layout doesn't match what you see in the pictures, that's absolutely fine.

TABLE OF CONTENTS

Usually, you'll want to start your journal with a table of contents page. As mentioned earlier, you don't need to decide which layouts you want to include, group your pages in any particular order, or figure out where they need to go in advance. But if you need to find a specific page, how would you look for it? This is where your table of contents comes in. It's simply a list of the pages in your journal along with the corresponding page number. You will continue to add more entries to the table of contents as you fill more pages.

»•→ TIP ←•«

Instead of setting up your table of contents as a simple vertical list, divide a two-page spread into columns. Label each column with a different category, such as School, Hobbies, and so on. As you're filling out your table of contents, add your entries to the appropriate column. This will allow you to easily find the pages that you're looking for, especially if your table of contents page is very long.

You can write down as many or as few entries in your table of contents as you like. For example, instead of making a separate listing for every planning page that you've made for July, you can simply write down the ones you refer to the most, or list all the page numbers in one line to save room.

PAGE NUMBERS

As discussed above, you'll need page numbers to help you navigate your journal. Many notebooks come with preprinted ones, but if yours doesn't, just handwrite them yourself.

MONTHLY LAYOUT

The monthly layout is dedicated exclusively for monthly planning. In many designs, you'll find a calendar alongside a list of scheduled events and things you need to do or want to accomplish. This list will serve as a reference as you plan your week or day and does not have to be very detailed. You'll have plenty of space to add specific details in your weekly and daily layouts. Feel free to start with any month—no need to wait until January!

>»•→ **TIP** ←•-«<

Because your journal does not have preprinted calendar pages, it can be difficult to keep track of events that are scheduled months in advance. Dedicate a page in your journal so you can write down these items. Just remember to flip back to this page whenever you start a new monthly layout to make sure you don't forget anything.

WEEKLY LAYOUT

Once you have your monthly layout ready to go, you'll then jump into the weekly layout. The weekly layout is any page that's used for weekly planning. Some weekly layouts offer a broad overview of the week's events, appointments, and to-do lists, while others include sections for each day of the week.

DAILY LAYOUT

You can plan out each day with a daily layout. Many daily page designs give you room to organize your day by the hour as well as jot down any other thoughts, observations, and notes that you might have. Some journalers who don't need a full page to organize their days opt to just use a weekly layout that outlines each day of the week in lieu of separate daily layouts. Give this a try if it sounds appealing.

HABIT TRACKERS

In between your monthly, weekly, and daily layouts, you might add habit-tracker spreads. These pages let you keep tabs on practices, activities, and tasks that you complete regularly (or want to complete regularly). Trackers give you the ability to record in a visual way how often you've done something over a set period of time. Some planning pages will also include miniature versions of full-page habit trackers.

PLANNING PAGES, LISTS, GALLERIES, AND MORE

You'll likely find yourself adding many pages that might not neatly fit into the categories listed previously. Some might be filled with lists related to a specific project (see "Project Planning Page," page 146), or you might choose to draw a spread designed to capture your favorite memories (see "Memory Gallery," page 136). Feel free to include as many specialized layouts as you like—the only limit is the number of pages in your notebook (and you can always find a new notebook when you run out of room).

CREATING AND ADAPTING YOUR LAYOUTS

BY ASHLYN MUESER

Creating and adapting layouts for my specific needs is one of my favorite things about journaling. With a blank page, you can design just about anything. You're open to endless possibilities; and while that may seem daunting at first, all you're really trying to do is figure out what works best for you. Sometimes you need a layout for a specific purpose and want to make something on your own. Other times you may see a design you like, but it doesn't quite suit your specific needs. For situations like these, here are some tips for creating and adapting layouts.

CREATING NEW LAYOUTS:

* First, make a list of the things you want to use your layout for. For example, when I created my weekly spread ("Categorized Task Lists," page 45), I knew I wanted ways to track exams and due dates, a place to write down study plans, and a place to note personal events and tasks.
* Sketch a rough design in pencil to ensure that all the elements of your spread fit on the page. Check that the overall layout addresses everything on your list. I always sketch before writing in pen to make sure that I like the layout and that I can see myself using it.
* Continue to tweak your sketch until you have a rough version of the layout you had in mind. It doesn't matter if it's messy. I'm always adjusting the size of boxes to make things more aesthetically appealing.
* Finally, use a pen and ruler to draw your layout on top of your rough, penciled layout. Wait for your ink to dry, erase your pencil lines, and voila! You've created your own layout.

ADAPTING OTHER LAYOUTS:

* Search for inspiration online or on social media sites. Always be sure to give credit to the original designer.
* If a layout that you like has sections for a specific purpose, rename those sections to match your needs. For example, my monthly layout ("Calendar-Style Layout," page 29) has spaces for due dates and exams because these dates were most important to me when I was a busy student. However, now that I've graduated, I use these spaces for birthdays and notes instead.

* If you find an idea you like, but the style isn't quite what you're looking for, follow the Creating New Layouts tips (on the previous page) with that idea in mind. For example, you may see the design for the Semester Overview (page 105) but not like the way the exam and assignment dates are arranged. Instead of just listing the dates, you could draw boxes that you can check off for each class or each month.

MAKING YOUR TO-DO LISTS

Now that you have a solid grasp of the basic backbone of your journal, it's time to move onto what actually goes on your pages: your to-do lists. At its simplest, creating a to-do list is easy—all you need to do is write down the things you need to do on a piece of paper, add new items when necessary, and check off anything that has been done. While organizing your tasks into a single running list is one way to approach your tasks, there are a few simple tricks to help your lists work more efficiently.

NEW PAGE, NEW LIST

When you create a new planning layout, you'll want to create a fresh to-do list, even if you haven't finished your old one. At first, writing a new list each and every day might sound like a lot of work, especially if you're writing the same tasks over and over again. However, making a new list gives you an opportunity to reflect and think about what you want to accomplish over a given timeframe. When you start paying attention to the items you've written down before, you'll start to see items that you no longer need to do or haven't even started yet. This gives you opportunity to refine your task list and think more deeply about what matters most at a particular moment.

MOVE UNFINISHED TASKS

There will inevitably come a time when you see some items on your list that you haven't gotten to yet. Never forget or leave them behind again! When you create your new to-do list, flip back to your old lists and note any unfinished, leftover tasks that you find. When you create a new list, transfer these remaining items over.

ASSIGN SYMBOLS

When you write down everything you need to do and remember in one giant list, it can be hard to tell what is high priority, no longer relevant, or simply not completed yet. The solution to this problem is simple: just assign a different symbol to categorize each task and indicate its status. There's nothing like a visual cue to help make your list more streamlined and easy to use.

Here are some examples of simple symbols that can work for any journal:

- ☐ Draw an open square next to your tasks.
- △ Draw an open triangle next to your events or appointments.
- ☐! Draw an exclamation point inside the squares or triangles for the high-priority items.
- ▲ For tasks that you've completed or events that have happened, fill in the corresponding shapes. You can fill in half of the shape if something is in progress.
- ⊿ For items that have not been completed at all or need to be rescheduled, draw an arrow.
- ⊠ For items that are no longer needed, draw a slash through the shapes.

You can create more symbols for specific types of items and experiment with different icons and abbreviations. For instance, for tasks that might require some additional research or follow up, draw a question mark inside your square. If you like jotting down ideas that come to you throughout the day, help them stand out by drawing a light bulb icon next to each one.

Once you've decided on your symbols, it might be a good idea to devote a page to a symbol directory, where you draw each symbol and write down a short description that explains what each one represents. This is especially helpful if you have a lot of them to remember, but if you have a good memory or a relatively simple set of symbols, you can save the page for something else.

DECORATING YOUR JOURNAL

Journaling can offer infinite opportunities to be creative, whether you're an artist who wants elaborate illustrations onto every page, a lettering enthusiast who experiments with *headers* (or the titles on each page), or someone who likes playing with simple geometric borders. Your journal can be an explosion of color or streamlined and minimalist. Every layout and individual element on the page is a chance to express your personal style.

But wait, you say. *Will journaling be a mistake if I have bad handwriting? Will my journal be boring if I just want simple pages? Will my journal be a failure if it's not a museum-worthy piece of art?* The answer to all three of these questions is no! How you choose to decorate your journal (or not) is a personal choice. Your journal can be as simple or complex as you want it be. If the thought of putting together a beautiful color-coded spread with detailed illustrations stops you in your tracks, remember that you don't need any embellishments for journaling to work for you. If your pages are filled with lists that are written with the random pen that you found at your desk, "decorated" with cross outs, and penned with your messiest handwriting, no one will bat an eye. In fact, they'll probably be impressed by how much you're getting done.

CHOOSING YOUR SUPPLIES

Now that we've gotten the set-up of your journal out of the way, it's time to gather your supplies. This quick guide will outline what you need and what to consider when you're choosing your notebook, writing utensils, and stationery supplies.

NOTEBOOK

It's easy to see with a quick online search or a trip to any paper-goods store that there's a lot to choose from when it comes to finding a notebook. Luckily, you can start journaling with just about any notebook, but there are a few things to keep in mind that will help you settle on one that will work the best for you.

Size

You'll want to choose a notebook that won't be too cumbersome to carry in your favorite bag yet large enough to fit everything that you want on a page without needing to adjust the size of your handwriting. If you're a first-time journaler,

an ideal size for your starter journal is about 6 × 8 inches (15.2 × 20.3 cm), or A6, if you're using a brand with European sizes, but you can also consider something pocket-size like 4 × 6 inches (10.2 × 15.2 cm), or go larger with a notebook that is 7 × 10 inches (17.8 × 25.4 cm).

Covers

Choose a journal with a sturdy cover that can withstand being poked, prodded, tossed, and dropped. Finding a waterproof journal might be a tall order, but if the cover has a coating or finish that can withstand a few drops of liquid or a small coffee spill, that's an added bonus. It's best to avoid notebooks with a paperback cover. Although they might be cheaper and lighter, they might not survive daily wear and tear.

Binding

For durability, notebooks with a sewn binding are your best choice. They'll be able to handle how often you'll be opening and closing your journal. Something that easily lies flat is helpful to have, and if a binding that lies completely flat is absolutely crucial, try a notebook with a spiral binding. If you go this route, be sure to choose a sturdy spiral that won't distort if it gets caught on something.

Extras

There are lots of bells and whistles that might make your journal even more useful. Closures are handy for keeping your journal in one piece, especially if you plan to take it with you everywhere you go, while ribbon markers are useful for retuning to frequently used pages or jumping right to your next clean page. Pen loops are a fun and functional touch for keeping your favorite writing utensil on hand, and for a convenient way to store loose scraps of paper, search for a journal with a pocket in its inside back cover. And if you want to keep things simple and skip these extra features? That's absolutely fine too.

Paper

Choose a journal with sturdy paper that is thick enough to avoid any bleed-through with your chosen writing utensil. If sustainably sourced paper is a priority, there are lots of options made from recycled materials or post-consumer waste.

As for what's printed on the page, you have lot of options, including dot grids, graph grids, lines, or completely blank pages. Pages with a rectangular grid or dot grid offer the benefit of providing you a preprinted guideline to use while you're writing or drawing on your pages. They're especially helpful when you're trying to draw straight lines, put together tables, or create a series of boxes that are the same size. All the page layouts in this book have been created with dot-grid paper.

If you're using a journal with blank pages, you can use a ruler and a little bit of math to help you create lines that are the same length as the ones in the layouts in this book. Most boxes on a dot-grid or graph paper are about ¼ inch (6 mm) square. You can multiply this measurement by the number of squares that are along the lines you want to draw. The number you calculate will equal the length of the line you should draw. For example, if you want to draw a line that is four squares long on a dot-grid page, multiply ¼ inch (6 mm) by 4; the line you'll draw on the blank page will be one inch (2.5 cm).

PENS

When it comes to choosing a perfect pen for your journal, the options are truly endless. There are different types of tips and inks and a rainbow of colors to choose from. Here's a quick overview of the most commonly used types, but no matter what you choose, remember that your writing utensil should be comfortable to use and easy to write with.

Pens are commonly measured based on the widths of their tips, which are measured in millimeters. You'll also find pens described as *fine point* or *extra-fine point*. The widths associated with these terms will vary, but as a general rule, *fine point* refers to a pen with a 0.7 mm tip, while *extra-fine point* refers to a pen with a 0.5 mm tip or smaller.

Ballpoint Pens

Ballpoint pens are probably the ones that come to mind when you think about pens. This type uses a tiny ball at its tip to dispense oil-based ink. You'll need to apply more pressure to write with a ballpoint pen, which could be a consideration if you plan to write a large amount of text in one sitting.

Rollerball Pens

If you want to a pen that writes more smoothly, consider a rollerball pen, which is a ballpoint pen with water-based ink. Because the ink is thinner and flows more easily, rollerball pens will create darker lines than your average ballpoint pens.

Gel Pens

Gel pens use the same kind of tip as ballpoint pens but dispense ink from a water-based gel. They also create vivid and bolder lines and come in a variety of colors—you can even find gel pens with metallic or glitter ink. Ink in gel pens can smudge more easily, so it's best to wait a second or two to let it dry before turning the page or touching anything that you just wrote.

Fine Line Drawing Pens

Also known as fineliners, fine line drawing pens feature fine, needle-like tips that are made from plastic and designed for precise line work. They often contain specially formulated ink that is more smudge-proof than the ink found in the other types of pens. Although they can be more expensive than rollerball or gel ink pens, they're a worthy investment if you're working on more detailed designs or if you simply want pens that write smoothly.

»∙—➤ TIP ◄—∙«

When it's time to shop for new pens, bring your journal on your next trip to the store and use a blank page in your journal for testing your writing utensils. You can learn right away whether the ink writes as smoothly as you like and check if the ink bleeds through your paper. If you find a specific brand and type that you like, write down its name and draw a line to create a writing sample. You'll soon have a visual reference for the way different inks and tips look on your page. Just be sure to check with the store's policy to see if they'll let you test their wares before purchasing them.

Felt-Tipped Pens

Felt-tipped pens have tips made from pressed fibers. They dispense ink that dries quickly and come in a wide range of colors, which make them useful for coloring small areas.

Brush Pens

As their name suggests, brush pens have a tip that mimics the range of motion of traditional brushes and lets you create thin and broad strokes. If you want to experiment with hand lettering in your journal, brush pens are great tools to have on hand.

COLORED PENCILS AND MARKERS

Add a splash of your color to your notebook pages or color-code your lists with a set of colored pencils and markers. A simple set with about a dozen colors will be more than enough. Double-ended markers are a great choice if you want both a thicker tip for creating large swaths of color and a finer tip for drawing lines or adding details to your layouts. If you're planning to keep your pages black-and-white, you can skip these items.

HIGHLIGHTERS

Don't forget about the humble highlighter! Highlighters usually dispense less ink than markers and leave a less saturated amount of color, making them a safe bet for journals with thinner paper or for emphasizing labels and headers.

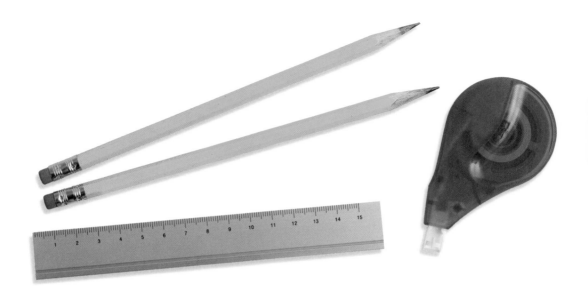

CORRECTION TAPE

Life is too short to stress about mistakes. Keep some correction tape at the ready for those inevitable cross outs or slips of the pen.

> **⋙•→ TIP ←•⋘**
>
> Did you make a mistake that your personal stash of correction tape can't handle? Just cover it up with a sticky note or some washi tape, and integrate it into the rest of your page design by writing an inspirational quote. No one will be the wiser!

PENCIL AND ERASER

If you want to avoid making mistakes in ink, be sure to include a pencil and eraser in your journaling toolkit. In fact, many of the instructions in this book recommend sketching your layouts first before finalizing them in pen.

RULER

Straight lines are easy to draw when you have a ruler at your disposal. A 6-inch (15 cm) ruler will be long enough to create most page layouts. The convenient size also makes it easy to take it with you if you plan to journal on the go.

STICKY NOTES

Sticky notes offer a way to quickly jot down a list or an important reminder without needing to worry where you're writing or what section your notes will fall into. You can always peel off your sticky notes when you no longer need them or move them to different pages.

STICKY PAGE FLAGS

Like sticky notes, sticky page flags are a versatile item in your journaling toolkit. Their smaller size make them perfect for bookmarking a page and or highlighting important information on your pages. They'll also be essential for the Reusable Meal Planner (page 121), where you'll use flags to jot down your favorite foods and plan out your dinners for the week.

STENCILS AND STAMPS

Hand drawing shapes like circles or letters and numbers can be time consuming, especially if you're copying the same design elements on many pages. You'll see some projects in this book recommend using stencils and stamps to save time. Many craft stores sell stamps for calendar grids, months of the year, days of the week, and more; if you're looking for something unique, you might find artists who design their own stickers as well. Stamps in particular are an easy way to add color and fun illustrations to your pages if drawing isn't in your wheelhouse.

STICKERS

Stickers are a great way to add some art or illustrations to your journal without needing to pick up a marker or pen. You can buy sheets of stickers that are designed specifically for planning; they often include the names of the months, days of the year, or fun icons and symbols.

USING STICKERS IN YOUR JOURNAL

BY MARIETHERES VIEHLER

If I had to choose only one thing out of my essentials for journaling (besides a notebook and a pencil, of course), it would definitely be my stash of stickers. It might sound silly. After all, why would an adult use stickers in a journal? Nonetheless, using stickers has made my life so much easier. Creating a spread now takes about ten minutes rather than an hour like it used to. Stickers are an awesome tool to highlight important notes, tasks, or events. Since stickers have been such a big part of my journaling journey I decided to design my own.

* Functional stickers like icons, flags, and days of the week help you instantly see important appointments or reminders.
* Decorating your journal with stickers is a lot easier and less time-consuming than drawing.
* Sticker kits with a specific theme can make your journal look very cohesive.

WASHI TAPE

This sturdy and semi-transparent tape is printed in a huge assortment of colors and patterns as well as a variety of widths. You can use washi tape to create an eye-catching border, divide your page into sections, add a fun banner to your page, or spruce up a plain notebook cover in record time.

⟫•→ TIP ←•⟪

If you want to write on your washi tape, avoid smudged ink by using a fine point permanent marker and letting the ink dry before closing your journal or touching your tape.

PAPER CLIPS AND BINDER CLIPS

Both paper clips and binder clips make convenient bookmarks and let you section off pages, which can be particularly useful if your notebook doesn't come with a ribbon marker. You can also use binder clips to hold the pages of your journal open while you're working. If your notebook doesn't have a pocket to store loose pieces of paper, you can turn one of the covers into a makeshift clipboard with a binder clip—just attach your clip to the top edge of the cover, and you're all set!

TIPS FOR GETTING STARTED FROM A SEASONED JOURNALER

BY CINDY THOMPSON

As a newbie journaler, I had so many ideas for what my journal would do for me. I was totally sure my plans would all pan out perfectly. Now, almost two years after I've ditched a preprinted planner, I've discovered some things I wish I had known when I was starting out. If I'd had these tips in mind when I cracked open my first journal, I would have saved myself some stress, at the very least. I hope that they do that for you.

* **Don't be afraid to make mistakes.** When I first started journaling, I was so afraid of making a mistake that it almost stopped me from starting at all. I thought a crooked line or a crossed-out word would ruin my journal, and I'd have to start over. Now, as a more seasoned journaler, my journal is filled with little mistakes, from measuring my lines incorrectly or drawing one in the wrong place to misspelling important things. Instead of letting these things "ruin" my journal, I use them as a challenge to test my creativity and help me think of ways to work around them. For example, I've learned that white gel pens work wonders for covering up accidental lines. The mistakes won't disappear completely, but they'll be a lot easier to look past.

* **Don't worry about getting it right the first time.** The beauty of journaling is the ability to evolve. You may think you know what you want your journal to look like, but until you start actually using it, you won't know what works and what doesn't. My daily entries have evolved and changed more times than I can count, even though I thought I had the perfect layout with my very first entry.

* **It's okay to change your mind.** If you find out that your journal layout or style isn't working, you can always change it. Sometimes making your journal look exactly like you want takes too much time for your lifestyle, and you need to make journaling easier to manage. Other times you might be bored and want to try something new. There is no bad reason to change up your journal.

* **Your journal doesn't have to look like anyone else's.** Your journal should be a reflection of you. While finding inspiration from outside sources is a great way to experiment, your journal ultimately serves your needs. You aren't doing it wrong if it doesn't look the same as someone else's. If what you're doing works for you, you're doing it right.

* **It's okay to take a break.** If you don't feel like journaling or don't have a need to journal for any amount of time, you are allowed to take a break. With a preprinted planner, you may feel like you are wasting pages when you take time off for a vacation, school break, illness, or any other reason, but with a blank journal, you get to stop and start back up without worrying about skipping anything.

* **Journaling should be fun.** When you find yourself frustrated with journaling or feeling obligated to put in hours of time that you don't enjoy, something is wrong. Journaling is a great hobby that happens to serve an organizational function, but if it isn't fun anymore, it's time to reassess. Whether that means simplifying or changing up your layouts, taking a closer look at which trackers are actually helping you, or just taking a little break from journaling, you should do what is right for you in the moment.

Page
Layouts

The lines within the date boxes correspond to the events listed in the sidebar. Add a line for each event happening on that date.

This sidebar gives you room to add important dates and sort them into individutal categories like the ones you see here.

3	4	5	6	7
10	11	12	13	14
17	18	19	20	21
24	25	26	27	28

september

8

impt
due

① math: fridays

② chem report
    9/7 & 9/21
③ bio paper
    9/18

exams

① BIO 141: 9/22

② math 140 quiz
    9/13
③ chem 110 quiz
    9/18

fun

① family visits
    9/22 - 9/24
② tailgate
    9/9
③ hiking 9/3

You can use color-coded symbols to represent various categories in the important dates section. I've used numbered circles in yellow for due dates, orange for exams, and pink for fun events.

Calendar-Style Layout

BY ASHLYN MUESER

This monthly layout is just like your everyday calendar and is great for recording all your events in an easy-to-see way, while still noting important items like due dates, exams, and fun events.

WHAT YOU'LL NEED

* Journal, one blank two-page spread
* Pencil and eraser
* Ruler
* Black brush pen
* Fine line black pens, 0.3 mm and 0.1 mm
* Gray fine point marker
* Fine point colored markers

WHAT YOU'LL DO

1 Using pencil, sketch your header. Write the name of the month across the bottom of the two pages. Feel free to add embellishments, like a quick doodle, and include the year.

2 Sketch the calendar. On the left page, draw a rectangle that fills the space above the header using pencil. Divide the rectangle evenly into four columns and five rows by drawing four horizontal and three vertical lines inside the edges. You should have twenty boxes. On the right page, draw a smaller rectangle with three columns and five rows. You should have fifteen boxes. The grid of the right rectangle should be aligned with the grid of the left rectangle.

3 Write the title for your sidebar in pencil. In this case, I have labeled it with an abbreviation of "Important." Underline your title.

4 Write in the names for each section of the sidebar with the pencil. Leave enough room between each name to write your tasks.

5 Draw in with pen all the lines sketched in Steps 2–4. For the header sketched in Step 1, use your black brush pen. For the remaining lines sketched in Steps 2–4, use the black 0.3 mm fine line pen.

6 After waiting a few minutes for the ink to dry, erase all pencil marks.

7 Using a gray fine point marker, write the dates in the boxes of the calendar. Depending on your preference, you can start your weeks on either Sunday or Monday. Draw diagonal lines through any boxes that will not contain a date.

8 Use the colored markers to add color to your page. You can color-code your tasks or add some decorations.

9 With the 0.1 mm drawing pen, fill in the sections of the sidebar with your tasks and events. Mark them on your calendar with the colored markers.

MAKE IT YOUR OWN!

* You can create sections in your sidebar for any important aspect of your life. For example, instead of recording due dates and exams, you can keep track of your workout routine.

* The size of the dates in each box can be changed to your liking. Some prefer smaller numbers in a corner; others may prefer larger, bolder numbers.

Two-Page Date List

BY MARIETHERES VIEHLER

This spread lists all of my dates and important events, while still giving me enough space to add details about my tasks and events. I keep the spread relatively simple to make sure that I will have time to set up and use it when I have a busy month. It requires just ten minutes to create.

WHAT YOU'LL NEED

* Journal, one blank two-page spread
* Pencil and eraser
* Ruler
* Black gel pen
* Stickers (optional)

WHAT YOU'LL DO

1 With your black pen, write the name of the month on the top of the left page.

2 With your pencil and ruler, sketch out one box at the bottom of each page. The bottom and top edges of the boxes should be a little narrower than the width of the page. My boxes are usually about a quarter of the page high, but you can make yours taller or shorter.

3 Decide how you want to divide the days of the month between the two pages. With your black pen, write the dates and the abbreviations for each day of the week down the left side of both pages. You will use these dates to plan out your month at a glance.

4 With the black pen, outline the edges of the boxes.

5 Erase any extra pencil marks. Make sure to let the ink dry to avoid smudging!

6 To use this spread, fill in any upcoming appointments and events next to the corresponding day of the month. For additional appointments that come up unexpectedly, ideas, or anything that springs to mind as the month goes by, use the boxes at the bottom of the pages to keep a running list of the things you want to remember.

MAKE IT YOUR OWN!

You can use this same template to create a simple gratitude page or write down a sentence or two about your day. The boxes at the bottom can provide space to review and write down the highlights of your month.

The numbers and letters on the left side of the page show the days of the week and the month.

october

1	S	
2	M	Journal video
3	T	Linkin Park concert
4	W	
5	T	
6	F	
7	S	Bank Appointment
8	S	Andrea's Birthday
9	M	
10	T	Workshop Meeting
11	W	
12	T	Yoga
13	F	Bills

to-do

- ■ Book Flights
- ☐ Journalspiration Stock
- ■ New Listings
- ■ Bills
- ☐ Health Insurance

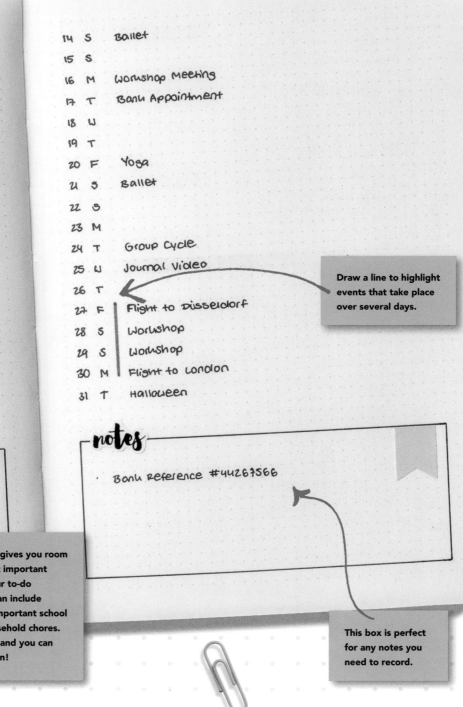

14	S	Ballet
15	S	
16	M	Workshop Meeting
17	T	Bank Appointment
18	W	
19	T	
20	F	Yoga
21	S	Ballet
22	S	
23	M	
24	T	Group Cycle
25	W	Journal Video
26	T	
27	F	Flight to Düsseldorf
28	S	Workshop
29	S	Workshop
30	M	Flight to London
31	T	Halloween

Draw a line to highlight events that take place over several days.

notes

- Bank Reference #44267566

This section gives you room for the most important tasks on your to-do list. These can include birthdays, important school events, household chores. You name it and you can write it down!

This box is perfect for any notes you need to record.

Journal

Draw small icons and symbols for every item to give you an overview of your schedule at a quick glance.

You can use the columns to write down events, appointments, personal tasks, reminders, or anything else relevant to your lifestyle.

November

events

personal

		events	personal
W	1		
T	2		• HAIR APPT. @ 4 PM.
F	3		• BUY GIFT FOR MOM
S	4	• ORCH. CONCERT @ 7 PM.	
S	5		✉ MAIL DOCUMENTS	• NAILS @ 3 PM.
M	6		
T	7	🎂 MOM'S BIRTHDAY	
W	8	• PRESENTATION @ 2 PM.	
T	9		• DENTIST APPT. @ 9 AM.
F	10		
S	11		
S	12		• RENEW PASSPORT
M	13		
T	14		• LUNCH W/ SARAH @ 1 PM.
W	15	👑 SAM'S BIRTHDAY	♡ 5 YEAR ANNIVERSARY ! - GIFT
T	16		
F	17	• CONFERENCE @ 5 PM	
S	18		
S	19		
M	20		
T	21	♡ 5 YEAR ANNIVERSARY !	
W	22		• HOME DECOR SHOPPING
T	23		
F	24	• NO SCHOOL	• REDECORATE BEDROOM
S	25		
S	26	• THANKSGIVING	$ PAY BILLS + BUDGET REVIEW
M	27	• MEETING W/ BRAD @ 1 PM.	
T	28		• PLAN FOR NEXT MONTH
W	29		
T	30		

30

⇥•→ **TIP** ←•⇤

If you find that you need more space to write down your tasks or events, you can continue this spread on the next page by adding more columns.

Two-Column Layout

BY CRISTINA TAMAS

This quick and simple monthly overview page is a great way to track events and personal tasks. Unlike the traditional calendar format, this two-column layout allows you to have a clear overview of your events and tasks separately so that you can locate each of them easily.

WHAT YOU'LL NEED

* Journal, one blank page
* Pencil and eraser
* Ruler
* Black fine line drawing pen
* Marker in any color with a thin and a wide tip
* White gel pen (optional)

WHAT YOU'LL DO

1 Starting from the bottom left of the page, write the days of the month in reverse order. Make sure you leave a column of space to the left of your numbers to write in the days of the week.

2 In the column to the left of each date, write the corresponding abbreviations for the days of the week. For example, *M* stands for *Monday*.

3 Using the wide tip of your colored marker, draw a bold horizontal line above the dates.

4 Using the thin tip of your colored marker, draw horizontal lines to separate the table into weeks.

5 With your pen, draw a vertical line down the middle of the table to split it into two columns.

6 Decide how you want to use each column, and label it accordingly.

7 For the header art, draw a thick line at the top of the page with the wide tip of your marker. Decorate this header line by drawing simple doodles on either side of it with your black drawing pen. To add extra details, use a white gel pen to add dots to the colored lines or outline the edges of the wide header line with the black drawing pen.

8 Finally, write the name of the month in the space between the header line and the table.

9 Fill in the spread with the upcoming events and tasks for each day and refer to this spread every day to make sure you stay on schedule. Ideally, you should create this spread at least a few days before the beginning of the month so that you can plan ahead.

MAKE IT YOUR OWN!

You can use this layout to track the stages of a specific project. All you need to do is change the labels of your columns to note tasks and dealines.

Linear Calendar

BY ERIN NICHOLS

With its linear calendar, this spread is simple to use and makes it easy to see all your monthly tasks at a glance. Unlike a traditional calendar, which can take much more time to create, this one-color spread is quick to put together and visually appealing. Along with plenty of room for recording events and appointments, it also has special sections for monthly tasks and notes.

WHAT YOU'LL NEED

* Journal, one blank page
* Pencil and eraser
* Ruler
* Black fine line drawing pen

WHAT YOU'LL DO

1 Orient the blank page to a landscape position. With your ruler, measure about one quarter of the page up from the bottom edge. Use the pencil to mark this distance. If your paper has a grid, the row with the pencil mark is where you will write the days of the month. If your paper is blank, then use your ruler and pencil to draw a row of squares to create a grid to write down the days of the month.

2 On the row you marked in Step 1, write out the days of the month with the black pen. Use one grid box for each day. To ensure that your calendar will be centered, locate the square at the center of the row. Write the number 15 in this box and write out the remaining numbers starting from here.

3 On the line above the days of the month, write the corresponding days of the week. You can abbreviate each day with just one letter, as I have done.

4 Use your ruler and black pen to draw a rectangle around the numbers and letters to create your linear calendar. Feel free to add some doodles or decorations around the edges of the rectangle or leave it plain.

5 At the top of the page, write the month in medium-large letters.

6 Use your ruler and black pen to draw a rectangle around the header. Add some geometric designs or illustrations for decoration if you wish.

7 In the right margin of the page, draw a tall box with your ruler and pen. Label the box *Notes*.

8 In the left margin of the page, draw another tall box with your ruler and pen. It should be the identical size as the right rectangle. Label it *Tasks*.

9 After you have added all of your headings and illustrations, erase any leftover pencil marks with your eraser.

10 To use the linear calendar, draw a vertical line straight up or down from the day you wish to add your event. Then make a small horizontal dash at the end of the line and write your event in next to it. You can add a dot at the end of the dash to make your event stand out more.

≫—●→ TIPS ←●—≪

* Use the space above your linear calendar for personal events and appointments and the bottom half for your work schedule.
* Need to write down multiple events on one day? Draw your line a little longer and add multiple horizontal dashes for separate events.

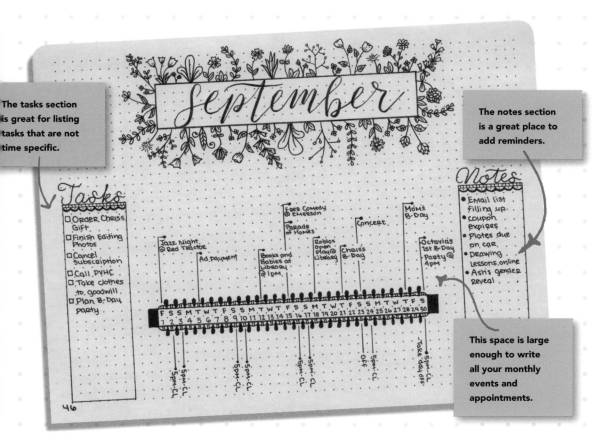

The tasks section is great for listing tasks that are not time specific.

The notes section is a great place to add reminders.

This space is large enough to write all your monthly events and appointments.

46

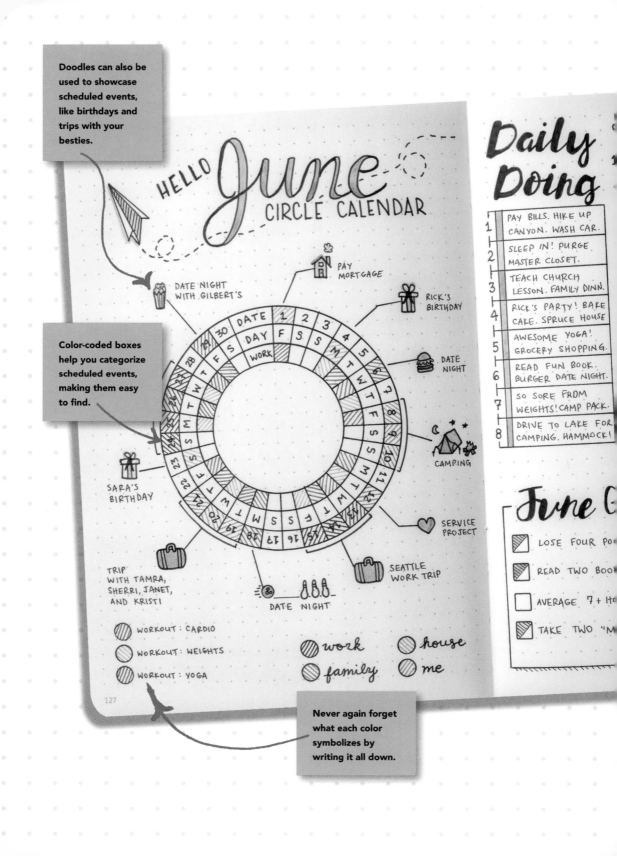

Doodles can also be used to showcase scheduled events, like birthdays and trips with your besties.

HELLO *June* CIRCLE CALENDAR

DATE NIGHT WITH GILBERT'S

PAY MORTGAGE

RICK'S BIRTHDAY

DATE NIGHT

CAMPING

SERVICE PROJECT

SEATTLE WORK TRIP

DATE NIGHT

SARA'S BIRTHDAY

TRIP WITH TAMRA, SHERRI, JANET, AND KRISTI

Color-coded boxes help you categorize scheduled events, making them easy to find.

DATE | 30 | DATE | 1 | 2 | 3 | 4 | 5 ...
DAY | F | S | DAY | F | S | S | M | T ...
WORK

WORKOUT: CARDIO
WORKOUT: WEIGHTS
WORKOUT: YOGA

work *house*
family *me*

Never again forget what each color symbolizes by writing it all down.

127

Daily Doing

1	PAY BILLS. HIKE UP CANYON. WASH CAR.
2	SLEEP IN! PURGE MASTER CLOSET.
3	TEACH CHURCH LESSON. FAMILY DINN.
4	RICK'S PARTY! BAKE CAKE. SPRUCE HOUSE
5	AWESOME YOGA! GROCERY SHOPPING.
6	READ FUN BOOK. BURGER DATE NIGHT.
7	SO SORE FROM WEIGHTS! CAMP PACK.
8	DRIVE TO LAKE FOR CAMPING. HAMMOCK!

June G

- [x] LOSE FOUR PO
- [x] READ TWO BOO
- [ ] AVERAGE 7 + H
- [x] TAKE TWO "M

Circle Calendar Spread

BY MICAH LEWIS

Creative journaling is all about finding useful and beautiful ways to display information that matters to you. Rather than using a traditional rectangular calendar to show your upcoming tasks, appointments, and events, how about drawing a circle instead?

WHAT YOU'LL NEED

* Journal, one blank two-page spread
* Pencil and eraser
* Ruler
* Large circle stencil or compass
* Black fine line drawing pens, in different widths
* Colored pencils
* Fine point colored markers

Wondering, "What on earth did I do all month?" Your journal can be the perfect place to write a few lines about what happened each day.

If you write down your goals and to-do tasks for the month, you're way more likely to get them done! Pinky swear!

AT
DOGS
20 | FIREWORKS

RIVE
CH.
21 | LATE FLIGHT HOME

M!
NEY
22 | SLEEP IN! DENTIST CHECK-UP.

CT!
PACK
23 | WORK PHOTO SHOOT. POST DESK FOR SALE!

! TOP
LE!
24

25

TON
HOME.
26

USE.
C.
27

CHURCH.
W/ RICK
28

MBA
G DATE
29

30

June TO-DO

2 | PURGE MASTER CLOSET
26 | MEETING WITH SUSAN
22 | DENTIST CHECK-UP
23 | WORK PHOTO SHOOT
23 | SELL DESK ONLINE
11 | LUNCH WITH COURTNEY

WHAT YOU'LL DO

Draw the Circle Calendar

1 On the top of the left page, draw a fun header to welcome the month.

2 Using the large circle stencil or compass and the pencil, draw one large circle in the center of the left page. Draw a smaller circle inside the larger one. You can add additional circles to create sections for specific items that you want to highlight, such as birthdays or assignments for class. {In this example, I added a circle for my workout routine.} Trace over your lines in pen when you're happy with shape and size of the circles.

3 With the ruler and pencil, draw diagonal lines through the circles to create the spaces for each day of the month and the labels for each ring. First, divide the circles into quarters, then divide each quarter into seven or eight sections, depending on the number days in the month. For each circle, there should be a section for each day of the month and one additional section for a label. Make sure the sections for your labels are large enough to write inside. Once you like the look of your sections, draw over the lines using your pen.

4 Fill the boxes in the outer circle with the days of the month and the corresponding smaller boxes in the second circle with the days of the week. Leave the boxes in the innermost circle blank to color-code later. Label each circle using the remaining empty boxes.

5 To jot down your appointments, holidays, events, and birthdays, write the name of each event near the date. Draw a fun doodle for each of your planned events, if you like. With your ruler and pen, draw a straight line connecting the name of the event and doodle with the date on the calendar.

6 To color-code your events, color in the boxes that correspond to events that you want to categorize together. You can also color in the boxes to highlight special events. For example, in my spread, I used orange for birthdays.

7 To remind you what each color symbolizes, write down the categories that you're using to organize your events on the bottom of the page. Draw small circles next to each one. Fill in each circle with the color used in the circle calendar.

Draw the Daily Doing Section

8 On the top left corner of the right page, create a fun label for your Daily Doing section. This is where you'll write a few sentences to summarize your day.

9 With the ruler and pencil, draw three long rectangles on the top two-thirds of the page. Place the left rectangle below the label.

10 Divide the rectangles into equal-size boxes for each day of the month with your pencil and ruler. Using your pen, label each box with the corresponding day. You can turn the numbers for each day of the month into

a fun border by drawing them along the left edges of your Daily Doing boxes.

11 When you're happy with the look of your boxes and labels, outline the pencil lines with the black pen. When the ink dries, erase any leftover pencil marks.

12 Use colored pencils and fine-point markers to add color and pizazz to each box!

13 Return to this spread daily to write a few lines about your busy day.

Draw the Goals and To-Do Sections

14 Beneath your Daily Doing boxes, draw two square boxes that fill the remaining space on the page. Label one box with *Goals* and the other with *To-Do*.

15 Draw little boxes inside each rectangle and list your goals and tasks for the month next to them. Prepare to check them off like a champ all month long. For items that you've made progress on, color in the boxes halfway to remind yourself to come back to them. If you've scheduled a date to complete some of the items, you can write the page number inside the box.

>>•→ **TIP** ←•«

Color isn't a requirement. Your journal can look amazing by just using black ink or one other color ink. Even if you don't have a color addiction like yours truly, small pops of color can still make a huge statement.

MAKE IT YOUR OWN!

Each ring in the circle calendar can be used to schedule specific time-sensitive items throughout the month, such as a social-media posts schedule, workout days, or due dates for homework assignments.

Use the weekly habit tracker to record how frequently you've completed recurring tasks or habits,

M T W T F S S

Make Bed
Quick Clean
Homemade Dinner

Hydration
Meditation
Workout
Supplements
Cleansing
Floss

Up 7am
Bed 11pm
Outside
No Snooze

to-do

Vacuum
Laundry
Bathroom
Change Sheets
Mop the Floors
Watering Flowers
Clean Brushes

M Chickpea Curry
T Mushroom Risotto
W Vegan Pizza
T Lentil Ragu
F Pea Soup
S Take Away
S Pasta with Pesto

we

3

M T W

M T W T

Write down one-off tasks in a separate to-do list.

This very simple meal planner is a nice add-on that makes it easier to start thinking about a shopping list and buying groceries for the week.

Running To-Do's

Bills
Upload new Listings
Call Bank
Prepare Giveaway
Answer to e-mails
Workshop
Journal Video
Refund
Book Flights London / Düssel.
Design Notebooks

> The running to-do list is perfect for any tasks you would like to complete within the upcoming week but aren't assigned a specific date. It also helps you understand why you tend to be more efficient on certain days.

Weekly Dashboard

BY MARIETHERES VIEHLER

This weekly layout is the perfect bridge between a monthly planning page and a daily planning page. It describes all the information from my monthly layout in a more detailed way with space to write down the most important tasks I need to do within the upcoming week. It incorporates a weekly habit tracker, which helps me stay on track and notice any possible patterns in my productivity. You can either use it for recurring tasks or change up the list every single week.

WHAT YOU'LL NEED

* Journal, one blank two-page spread
* Pencil and eraser
* Ruler
* Black gel pen, 0.38 mm
* Colored brush pen
* Black brush pen (optional)
* Open circle stamp and black inkpad (optional)
* Stickers (optional)

WHAT YOU'LL DO

1 With the black gel pen, write down the habits that you want to track at the top of the left page. You can group the habits into categories or just create a running list.

2 Leave a space below your last entry. Beneath that space, start writing down the individual tasks that you want to accomplish during the week.

3 Across from your to-do list, add your meal plan in a separate column. If you're not sure what you want to eat yet, you can just write the abbreviations for each day and fill in the meal planner later.

4 Use the circle stamp and inkpad to make the circles for the habit trackers and the to-do list. For the habit tracker, place seven circles across each habit for every day of the week, leaving a space between each circle. For the to-do list, place the circle to the left of each task. You will fill in these circles when you complete a task or practice a habit. If you don't have a stamp, you can draw the circles by hand.

5 Add a "to-do" sticker on top of your to-do list. You can also write the label with a brush pen.

6 On the right page, add your header to the top section. I start with a wreath sticker. Inside the sticker, I like to write down the week in a cursive font to make it stand out from the rest of the layout. You can draw a similar design for your header or create your own.

7 Below your header, create the columns for your running to-do list. Starting from the left side of the page, write down the letters to symbolize each day of the week. Leave a small space and then write *Running To-Do's*. You can use a marker to highlight these labels.

8 Under the *Running To-Do's* label, write down the tasks that you want to get done. To assign dates for these tasks, draw a box underneath the corresponding day of the week in the left column. When you've completed your task, you can fill in the box. The dots at the end of a finished task are optional, but they make it easier to connect the box with the specific task on the list at the right. If you decide to move a task to another day, draw a box under the new day.

9 Erase all the extra pencil marks. Make sure to let the ink on the page dry to avoid any smudging!

TIPS

* The space for the running to-do list can also be used for notes or longer to-do lists. You can change the type of list you use every week, depending on what you need to remember.
* If you need more space for all your weekly habits, skip the to-do list and meal plan on the bottom of the left page.

WEEKLY PLANNING

Categorized Task Lists

BY ASHLYN MUESER

Rather than splitting tasks by day, this layout divides them into categories to help keep your personal life separate from schoolwork. This way, you can hone in on certain items as needed, without the exciting distraction of personal events.

WHAT YOU'LL NEED

* Journal, one blank two-page spread
* Pencil and eraser
* Ruler
* Black fine line pens, 0.3 mm and 0.1 mm
* Black brush pen
* Fine point colored markers

WHAT YOU'LL DO

1 Using the pencil, sketch the header for both pages. The header on the left page should indicate the date range for the week, and the header on the right page should indicate the week number.

2 With the pencil and a ruler, draw the boxes for each task category that you want to include. The size of each box will depend on how much room you'll need for your to-do lists. To make your layout look neat and orderly, it's best to draw boxes that are either the entire width of the page or half of it.

3 With the pencil, write in the labels for the box titles on the top edge of the boxes.

4 Using the pencil, feel free to add some doodles on the edges of your boxes.

5 Erase any pencil lines that run beneath the box titles or intersect the doodles. You can let the edges of the boxes touch the headers, but erase the ends of the pencil lines near the doodles to leave a little space between the edges and your drawings.

6 Draw in all the lines sketched in Steps 1–5 with pen. For the header sketched in Step 1, use your black brush pen. For the remaining lines sketched in Steps 2–5, use the black 0.3 mm or 0.1 mm fine line pen. (The image shows doodles drawn using the 0.3 mm pen.)

7 After waiting a few minutes for the ink to dry, erase any visible pencil marks.

8 Add some color by underlining the header and outlining your doodles with the markers.

9 Fill in each section of the layout with your tasks and events using the 0.1 mm drawing pen. Completing this layout early, preferably the week before or the weekend before, will help you keep up with your to-do list.

MAKE IT YOUR OWN!

The spread you see here has been adapted for a student who wants to keep track of schoolwork and exams, as well as a personal to-do list and social events, in one place. All of these sections can be adjusted to match your personal needs. Simply change the headers to whatever tasks you want to organize! For example, if you want it to reference your work life, switch out the headers on the left page to these instead: *Meetings*, *Travel Plans*, and *Upcoming Deadlines*.

This space gives you room to write down the assignments you must complete that week.

You can create a designated section for outlining a study plan and a time line for assignment completion.

sepr

to complete

- hw 1 - thurs
- hw 2 - fri
- report 1 - wed
- hw 2 - fri
- lab 1 - tues
- hw 1 - tues
- report - fri

study/assi

m·o·n:
- study - quiz
- hw 1 - start
- study - exam
- lab 1 - work on

t·u·e·s:
- hw 1 - finish
- report 1 - work on
- lab 1 - finish
- hw 1 - start
- study - quiz
  \ exam

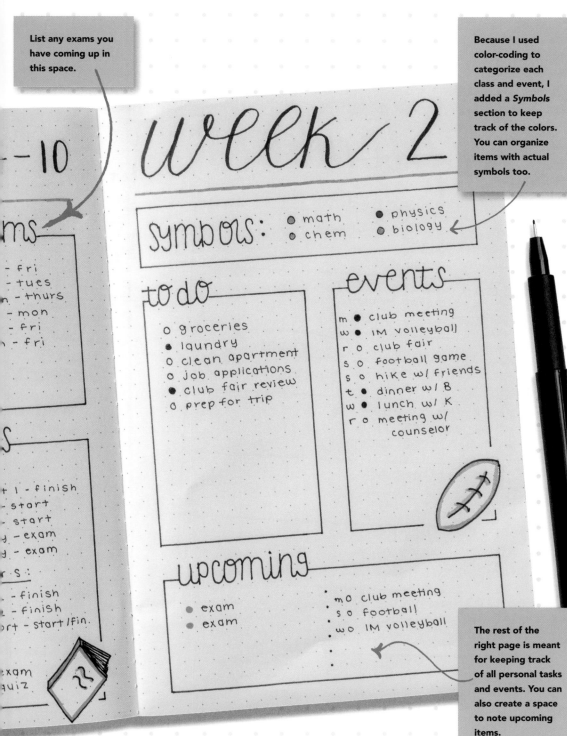

List any exams you have coming up in this space.

Because I used color-coding to categorize each class and event, I added a *Symbols* section to keep track of the colors. You can organize items with actual symbols too.

The rest of the right page is meant for keeping track of all personal tasks and events. You can also create a space to note upcoming items.

week 2

symbols: ● math   ● physics   ● chem   ● biology

to do

- o groceries
- ● laundry
- o clean apartment
- o job applications
- ● club fair review
- o prep for trip

events

- m ● club meeting
- w ● IM volleyball
- r o club fair
- s o football game
- s o hike w/ friends
- t ● dinner w/ B
- w ● lunch w/ K
- r o meeting w/ counselor

upcoming

- ● exam
- ● exam

- m o club meeting
- s o football
- w o IM volleyball

September 4/10

schedule

4
M

5 □ Ad payment
  □ transfer to bank

T

Family movie night

7 □ Clean out email
  □ Clean car

T

8 □ Run all errands

F

9 □ Work 5-CL

S

10 □ Work 5-CL

S

8

Tasks

MTWTFSS
□ Lay
□ Clea
□ Floc
□ Wat
□ Gro
□ Pos
□ Kid
□ Bil
□ Ch
□ Yoc

□ New KG songs
□ Talk to Doc abou
□ Quote stickers f
□ Music for wedding

BRAIN

Mon:
- Buy Milk

Tue:
- Buy stuffed shell
  ingredients
- Insurance Renewa
  end of Month

Vertical Weekly Schedule

BY ERIN NICHOLS

This spread is ideal if you want to add a full page of special sections to your layout, like space for tracking tasks or a "brain dump" area for jotting down anything on your mind. It's easy to see all of your plans in one place, and the design of the second page is completely flexible. You can pick and choose the elements that match your needs.

WHAT YOU'LL NEED

* Journal, one blank two-page spread
* Pencil and eraser
* Ruler
* Black fine line drawing pen
* Pastel marker
* Colored fine line drawing pens

The Tasks chart is a fun and efficient way to visualize what you need to accomplish each day. Because the weekly boxes are narrow, I like to use this for recurring tasks. This way, they don't crowd the weekly boxes.

In the Next Week section, you can write down any important appointments, deadlines, or events for the upcoming week.

Use the Notes section to record important details to keep in mind for each day, such as what you need to buy at the grocery store, upcoming schedule changes, and bills that are coming due.

M T W T F S S
1 2 3
4 5 6 7 8 9 10
11 12 13 14 15 16 17
18 19 20 21 22 23 24
25 26 27 28 29 30

Next Week

□ Project deadline.
□ CC Payment due
□ Take Kids to Library.
□ DATE NIIE!

Notes

ses Sun
Babysitter
Blog Spread.

for FB Board
parkling water.

WHAT YOU'LL DO

1 On the left page, use the ruler and pencil to draw a large rectangle for the weekly schedule. Make sure you leave enough room at the top of the page for the header.

2 Divide the rectangle into seven equal-size sections by drawing six horizontal lines inside the rectangle. Each day should have the same amount of space.

3 Along the left side of each section, use your black pen to write the letter of the corresponding day.

4 Trace the remaining edges of the rectangle with your black pen, leaving any pencil lines that intersect the letters for the days of the week. Erase these stray pencil marks when the ink is dry.

5 Create your header above the finished weekly schedule. The header should include the month and the days of the week this page will cover.

6 Use your pastel marker to highlight the header and the days of the week in the schedule.

Draw the Task List

7 On the right page, create a small *Tasks* header on the top left side.

8 Under the header, starting from the left, write the letter abbreviations of each day of the week.

9 Move your pen below the days of the week and to the right. Starting at this point, write out recurring tasks you want to complete this week.

10 Under the days of the week, draw boxes on the days you would like to complete a specific task. In my example, I want to do laundry on Monday and Friday, so I put a box under *M* and *F* on the *Laundry* line.

11 Continue doing this until you have drawn in boxes for all your tasks. When you're finished, draw straight lines through the empty spaces with the black pen.

12 As the week progresses, fill in the boxes with colored pens as you complete your tasks.

> **»·•→ TIP ←•·«**
>
> Use color-coding to categorize tasks and events. I used seven different colors to represent the days of the week. For example, all tasks completed on Monday are struck through with light purple.

Draw the Mini Calendar

13 Move to the upper-right corner of the right page. Create a mini calendar of the current month using your black pen. No need to draw lines here—your numbers will create a grid.

14 Use your pastel marker to highlight the current week you're planning.

Draw the Next-Week Section

15 Below the mini calendar, write *Next Week*.

16 Draw a box underneath the words. You can draw a closed rectangle or leave the right side open and embellish the lines as I did in mine.

17 Add any events or appointments that will occur next week in the box.

Draw the Brain-Dump Section

18 Under your Tasks list, draw a large cloud shape with your black pen. Trace the inside of it with your pastel marker.

19 Use this space to record anything you want.

Draw the Notes Section

20 At the bottom of the page, use your ruler to draw a large horizontal box and label it, *Notes*.

21 Use this section to add daily notes. You can add a heading with the day of the week within the box, and then add shorthand notes under the heading. This can include shopping lists, people you need to call, and so on.

HOW TO CREATE DECORATIVE HEADERS

BY EMMA BRYCE

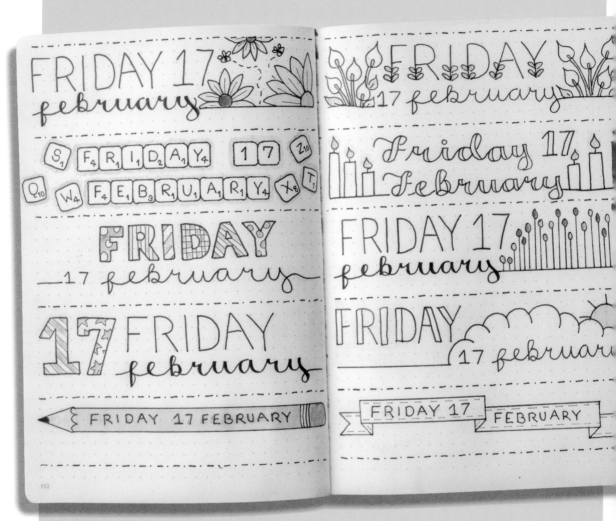

When I first started keeping a journal, I wanted to use it as a way to be organized and as a creative outlet. During the first week of journaling, I drew the date in a different style each day, and I just never stopped! I find inspiration from all around me— the news, notable events, even the washing on the line. My favorite theme that I have ever done was The Twelve Days of Christmas for December. Have fun trying some daily doodles with this quick tutorial!

WHAT YOU'LL NEED

* Pencil
* Fine line black drawing pens in various widths
* Eraser
* Colored pencils and pens

WHAT YOU'LL DO

1 Pick a theme for your header. It can be related to a holiday, season, or the weather, or you can choose something generic, like a banner design.

2 Write the date in your chosen font in pencil. On left pages, I tend to have the date positioned on the left or center of the page, and on right pages, I place it either at the center or aligned to the right. The choice is yours! You can also choose any font you like, I often look online or in magazines for inspiration. To start, you can try cursive, bubble writing, calligraphy, or tall capital letters. If necessary, erase and rewrite the characters until you are happy with them.

3 Sketch your decorations and doodles around the letters in pencil.

4 Outline the whole thing with the black pen. Once the ink dries, erase any pencil marks.

5 Color your decorations with the pencils and pens.

Decorate your headers with anything relating to that day, season, or planned event.

Use the space beneath your header to fill in any notable events, appointments, and tasks.

monday 17th JULY

- ☒ Gym with Sharla
- ☒ Wash gym kit
- → Write up meeting notes

tuesday 18 july

- ☒ 18:30 dinner with Mel

WEDNESDAY 19th july

- ☒ Start holiday packing
- Pay bills

Draw some boxes in each section to fill in your plans. To save time, I draw them when I first set up the week, but you can always add boxes as you go along.

19:

- ☒ Jes

Satu

- ☒ Sk

Sunc

- ☐ f
- ☒ L

72

SDAY 20
ULY

FRIDAY
21 JULY

day

WEEKEND

Lisa and Amanda

r

73

Layout with Decorative Headers

BY EMMA BRYCE

This weekly layout works well for me as it has enough space in each section to write down all my appointments and any events and things I need to remember. Keep this spread bright and personal with individual headers for each day. Illustrate each one with drawings of objects, plants, buntings, or banners relating to your day.

WHAT YOU'LL NEED

* Journal, one blank two-page spread
* Pencil and eraser
* Ruler
* Fine line black drawing pens in various widths
* Colored pencils

WHAT YOU'LL DO

1 Using a fine line pen and ruler, split your two-page spread into six equal sections. (I only do one header for the weekend.) Experiment with different decorative elements to separate each section, such as dotted lines, zigzag lines, dots, or dashes.

2 To create the headers, write the dates for each day in the week at the top of each section. Use your pencil to experiment with size, different fonts, and layouts. (For instructions, see "How to Create Decorative Headers," pages 52–53.) Don't be afraid to erase and start again.

3 Using your pencil, decorate each section appropriately for the day, season, or event you are going to.

4 Once you are happy with the layout, use your fine line pens to outline. Let the ink dry, then gently rub away your pencil marks with the eraser.

5 Color in your decorations with colored pencils. Add in any final detail with the fine line pens.

6 To use this spread, just fill in your plans for the week. Draw boxes for each task, event, or appointment and then check them off when completed. I set it up on a Sunday night and keep filling in the sections as needed throughout the week. You can set up these spreads a few weeks in advance to get ahead!

> »⟶ **TIP** ⟵«
>
> Keep an easy-to-reference list of notable dates or holidays that would be fun to illustrate, such as a birthday, graduation, the Fourth of July, or Halloween. You can put this list on a page in the back of your journal.

Horizontal Weekly Layout

BY CRISTINA TAMAS

This structured spread will help you organize your weekly schedule, prioritize your tasks, and record your expenses, meals, and shopping list. It has space that allows you to quickly and easily plan each day of the week.

WHAT YOU'LL NEED

* Journal, one blank two-page spread
* Pencil and eraser
* Ruler
* Black fine line drawing pen or any pen of your choice
* Colored markers and pencils

WHAT YOU'LL DO

1 With your pencil, divide each of your two pages into six equal-size sections. You will have twelve sections in total.

2 Using pencil lines as reference, draw eight equal-size boxes with a pencil and ruler. Place one box in each of the six sections on the right page. The remaining two boxes go in the sections on the top of the left page. You will use one box for each day of the week and one for the Shopping List.

3 In the top left section of the left page, write the week number. You can draw horizontal lines above and below it to help it stand out.

4 Underneath the week number, draw a small monthly calendar with your black pen. Use your marker to highlight the current week.

5 Below the calendar, draw three boxes of the same size with your pencil and ruler.

6 Fill in the remaining space on the bottom of the left page with a large box. Align the edges with the edges of the boxes surrounding the space.

7 Outline the boxes with your fine line black drawing pen. Once the ink is dry, erase any extra pencil marks.

8 In one of the small boxes beneath the calendar, write down the types of tasks that you want to track, and draw a colored box next to each item using your pen and markers. Label the other two small boxes *Goals* and *Important*. Label the remaining boxes *Notes*, *To-Do's*, and *Shopping List*. Feel free to highlight your labels with marker.

9 Divide the boxes for the days of the week into six cells, as seen in the photo.

10 In the top left cell of each box, write in the date. In the cell below the date, write the hours that you want to track and plan around. Divide the hours into two rows. In my spread, the hours span from 6:00 a.m. to 9:00 p.m.

11 Dedicate a few minutes the night before or in the morning to planning for the day and writing down your tasks in the cell below the time tracker. This way, you'll start the day with a clear plan in mind and you'll know which items need to be checked off your list. At the end of the day, fill in the expenses section and in the last cell of the box, write down what you've eaten. Don't forget to highlight the hours that you spent on your tasks on your time tracker using markers in the assigned colors.

MAKE IT YOUR OWN!

You can divide the daily boxes into as many or as few sections as you need and assign them any purpose that you like. Create spaces for reminders, notes, quotes, or daily reflections.

This time tracker provides a visual overview of your daily schedule. The numbers represent the hours in a day. You can use color to help you see when certain activities begin and how much time they take.

Use this section to record the colors that you'll be using in your time tracker and what they stand for.

Record top-priority tasks here.

WEEK 39

M T W T F S S
          1
2 3 4 5 6 7 8
9 10 11 12 13 14 15
16 17 18 19 20 21 22
23 24 25 26 27 28 29
30 31

MORNING ROUTINE
WORK / BUSINESS
HOUSEWORK / ERRANDS
MEETINGS / APPTS.
GOING OUT / RELAX

GOALS

O MAKE TIME FOR HOBBIES
● DRINK MORE WATER
● TRY A NEW RECIPE
O ONE DAY AT A TIME!

IMPORTANT

● PAY ELECTRICITY BILL
● SCHEDULE DENTIST
O PROJECT REVIEW

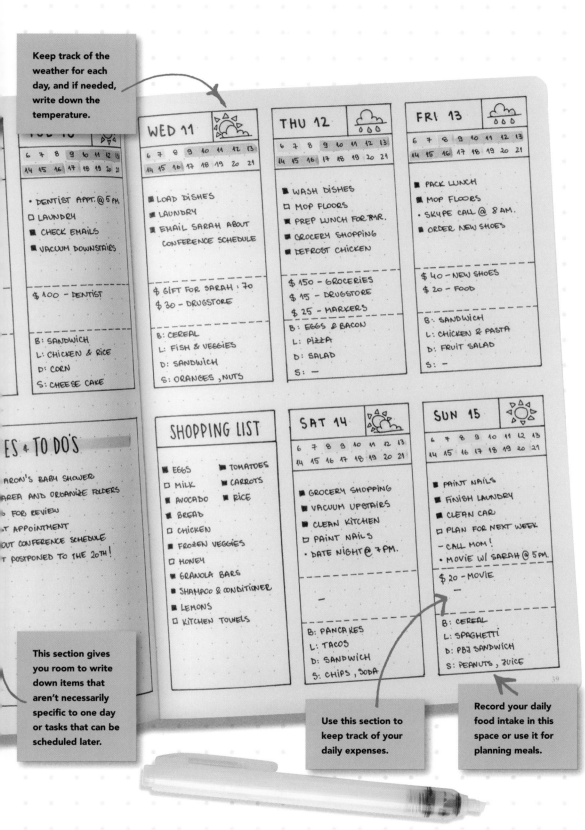

Keep track of the weather for each day, and if needed, write down the temperature.

TUE 10

6 7 8 9 10 11 12 13
14 15 16 17 18 19 20 21

- DENTIST APPT. @ 5 PM.
- ☐ LAUNDRY
- CHECK EMAILS
- VACUUM DOWNSTAIRS

$ 100 - DENTIST

B: SANDWICH
L: CHICKEN & RICE
D: CORN
S: CHEESE CAKE

WED 11

6 7 8 9 10 11 12 13
14 15 16 17 18 19 20 21

- LOAD DISHES
- LAUNDRY
- EMAIL SARAH ABOUT CONFERENCE SCHEDULE

$ GIFT FOR SARAH : 70
$ 30 - DRUGSTORE

B: CEREAL
L: FISH & VEGGIES
D: SANDWICH
S: ORANGES, NUTS

THU 12

6 7 8 9 10 11 12 13
14 15 16 17 18 19 20 21

- WASH DISHES
- ☐ MOP FLOORS
- PREP LUNCH FOR TMR.
- GROCERY SHOPPING
- DEFROST CHICKEN

$ 150 - GROCERIES
$ 15 - DRUGSTORE
$ 25 - MARKERS

B: EGGS & BACON
L: PIZZA
D: SALAD
S: —

FRI 13

6 7 8 9 10 11 12 13
14 15 16 17 18 19 20 21

- PACK LUNCH
- MOP FLOORS
- SKYPE CALL @ 8 AM.
- ORDER NEW SHOES

$ 40 - NEW SHOES
$ 20 - FOOD

B: SANDWICH
L: CHICKEN & PASTA
D: FRUIT SALAD
S: —

ES & TO DO'S

- ARON'S BABY SHOWER
- AREA AND ORGANIZE FOLDERS
- S FOR REVIEW
- T APPOINTMENT
- OUT CONFERENCE SCHEDULE
- T POSTPONED TO THE 20TH !

This section gives you room to write down items that aren't necessarily specific to one day or tasks that can be scheduled later.

SHOPPING LIST

- EGGS
- ☐ MILK
- AVOCADO
- BREAD
- ☐ CHICKEN
- FROZEN VEGGIES
- ☐ HONEY
- GRANOLA BARS
- SHAMPOO & CONDITIONER
- LEMONS
- ☐ KITCHEN TOWELS
- TOMATOES
- CARROTS
- RICE

SAT 14

6 7 8 9 10 11 12 13
14 15 16 17 18 19 20 21

- GROCERY SHOPPING
- VACUUM UPSTAIRS
- CLEAN KITCHEN
- ☐ PAINT NAILS
- DATE NIGHT @ 7 PM.

—

B: PANCAKES
L: TACOS
D: SANDWICH
S: CHIPS, SODA

Use this section to keep track of your daily expenses.

SUN 15

6 7 8 9 10 11 12 13
14 15 16 17 18 19 20 21

- PAINT NAILS
- FINISH LAUNDRY
- CLEAN CAR
- ☐ PLAN FOR NEXT WEEK
- — CALL MOM !
- MOVIE W/ SARAH @ 5 PM.

$ 20 - MOVIE
—

B: CEREAL
L: SPAGHETTI
D: PBJ SANDWICH
S: PEANUTS, JUICE

59

Record your daily food intake in this space or use it for planning meals.

June
THIRD-NINTH
week no. 23

S	M	T	W	T	F	S
					1	2
3	4	5	6	7	8	9
10	11	12	13	14	15	16
17	18	19	20	21	22	23
24	25	26	27	28	29	30

weekly to-do
- ☑ CALL GRANDPA
- ☑ WASH CAR
- ☑ WEED GARDEN
- ☑ ICE CREAM SOCIAL
- ☐ PACK FOR SEATTLE

- ◑ work
- ◑ family
- ◑ house
- ◑ me

The Weekly To-Do List features tasks that need to be completed throughout the week. I pull from this list to fill in tasks in the Daily Boxes.

The tasks are color-coded based on the four colors listed in the legend on the left page.

123

sunday (3)
- ☑ CHURCH
- ☑ FAMILY DINNER
- ☑ BOARD GAMES (KYLE WON!)

F U N
8   3   2

💧 ○○○○○○○

wednesday (6)
- ☑ WORK CONFERENCE CALL
- ☑ NEXT WEEK'S MEAL PLANS
- ☑ BASEBALL GAME

💧 ○○○○○○○○

saturday (9)
- ☐ PACK FOR SEATTLE
- ✓ SEATTLE WORK TRIP!

💧 ○○○○○○○○○

The tracker at the bottom of each day shows a drop of water and circles to fill in as a reminder to stay hydrated.

monda
- ◑ GRANDPA
- ☑ GET CA
- ☑ CALL GR
- ☑ WEEKLY

💧 ○○

thursc
- ♡ DATE
- ☑ PLAN
- → MOP

💧 ○

weather
task
- MAKE B
- WALK
- BREA
- DISHE
- WASH
- FLOSS
- SPEN
Habits

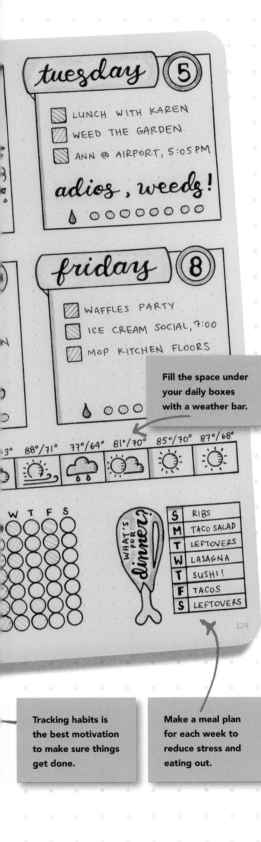

Fill the space under your daily boxes with a weather bar.

Tracking habits is the best motivation to make sure things get done.

Make a meal plan for each week to reduce stress and eating out.

Horizontal Weekly Layout Variation

BY MICAH LEWIS

You can plan and track what's happening in your world using this weekly spread, which also shows the days of the week, weather, weekly goals, and even what's on the menu for dinner. Not only do I love seeing my week from this perspective, it has also been a huge creative outlet.

WHAT YOU'LL NEED

* Journal, one blank two-page spread
* Pencil and eraser
* Ruler
* Black fine line drawing pens, in different widths
* Colored pencils
* Colored fine point markers

WHAT YOU'LL DO

Draw the Header, Monthly Calendar, Weekly To-Do List, and Legend

1 Using a pen, create your header in the top left corner of the left page. It should include information about the month and week.

2 Underneath your header, draw a small monthly calendar. You can simply write the days in rows that correspond to each week in the month. Feel free to start each week of the calendar with Monday instead of Sunday if that floats your boat! Color in the week of the month being shown in this particular spread.

3 With the pen and ruler, draw a box below your monthly calendar for your weekly to-do list. Write down the items that need to be completed this week but that do not need to be assigned to a specific day. Draw boxes next to each item. You can reference this list each day when you have free time to make sure everything gets done. Fill in the boxes as each task gets completed. I use a color assigned for that specific day, so I know which day of the week I finished that task.

4 Below your weekly to-do list, create your legend. List the different types of events and tasks that are happening throughout the week and assign each type a color.

TIP

You might not always need a legend to show your color-coding, especially after you start using the same colors for a few weeks. You can fill the extra space with inspirational quotes or a health tracker.

Draw the Daily Boxes

5 Using the pencil and ruler, sketch seven boxes across the two pages for your days of the week. When you are ready to make the boxes permanent, outline the side and bottom edges of each box with the black pen.

6 Label each box. On the top edge of each box, create a banner with the day of the week using your pen. Draw a circle next to your banner and write the date inside the circle. With the pen, outline any remaining pencil lines. Once the ink is dry, erase any stray pencil marks.

7 Fill each box with the day's tasks. Draw doodles in each box to highlight special events, like drawings of a party hat to celebrate a birthday or sushi for date night. In the bottom of each box, draw a teardrop and a row of circles to create a water-intake tracker to prove you're drinking enough each day! The number of circles should correspond to the amount of water that you want to drink each day.

8 Color-code each day to stay organized. Keeping the days of the week color-coded throughout your journal is a great way to track progress on bigger, monthly spreads. Color the banners on the top of each box using the color that you assigned for the day. I use blue for Sunday, pink for Monday, purple for Tuesday, and so on.

Draw the Trackers and Meal Planner

9 Create the weather bar. On the bottom of the right page, draw a label that reads *Weather*. Add a doodle if you like. With your pen and ruler, draw a rectangle next to your header. Divide the rectangle into seven sections of equal size. Each section will correspond to a day of the week.

10 Underneath the weather bar, create a weekly habit tracker. With a pen and ruler, draw a column of boxes on the left side of the page. The number of boxes in the column should correspond with the number of habits that you want to track. Fill in each box with your chosen habits. Add seven circles to the right of each box for each of day of the week. As you practice these habits throughout the week, fill in the circles with lines, little dots, X marks, or checks.

11 In the lower right corner of the page, draw a simple table with two columns and seven rows for your weekly meal plan using your ruler and pen.

12 With your colored pencils and markers, make any drawings that you've added pop off the page.

⤜•→ TIP ←•⤛

Don't beat yourself up if you have a week when you don't fill in as many tasks and habits. The beauty of this type of journaling is that each day is a fresh start! You can try again tomorrow and do even better than today. See the good in yourself first, and it will shine for others to enjoy as well.

tuesday

8

9 · clean the Flat

10 · Customer service

11 · Prepare Workshop
Meeting

12

1

2 Workshop Meeting

3

4

5 · Design Monthly Kit

6

7 · Dinner

8

9 · Upload Monthly Kit

10 · Prepare Giveaway

11

important

- ☑ order new Paper
- ☐ Bank Appointment
- ☑ Bill
- ☑ Monthly Kit

notes

Giveaway:
- · Gel Pen
- · Sticker Kit
- · Brush Pens

I use this *Important* section to write down high-priority goals and tasks. It helps me focus on just a few things that need to be accomplished on a particular day.

Blocking out appointments and events on the time line makes it easy to see periods of free time instantly.

The second box is perfect for any notes you might need to write down.

Vertical Time Line

BY MARIETHERES VIEHLER

This spread is by far the most important for me because I use it on a day-to-day basis. Since my very first attempts at journaling, I've always used a time line when I had busier weeks ahead of me. It especially helps me remember my appointments and to-do list and schedule my day down to the hour and doesn't take much time to put together.

WHAT YOU'LL NEED

* Journal, one blank page
* Pencil and eraser
* Ruler
* Black gel pen
* Colored brush pen
* Black brush pen (optional)
* Stickers (optional)

WHAT YOU'LL DO

1 For the daily header, write down the day of the week with your brush pen, or use a sticker. To make it stand out, you can add a strip of color using the marker.

2 Below the header, write down the hours of the day on the left of the page to create the time line. I start the day at 8:00 a.m. and end it at 11:00 p.m., but you can change the time span depending on your personal preferences.

3 On the right side of the page, draw two boxes with your pencil. When you are happy with the size and placement of the boxes, outline their edges in pen.

4 Label the top box *Important* and the other *Notes*. You can hand-letter the labels with a brush pen or use stickers.

5 Erase all the extra pencil marks. Make sure to let the ink on the page dry to avoid any smudging!

6 To use the time line, write the tasks and appointments next to their scheduled times or the times that you feel you can complete them. To block off specific periods, draw and fill in a narrow rectangle next to the corresponding time slot.

MAKE IT YOUR OWN!

It's always possible to change the sections on the right of the page to write down other items like your goals, workout plans, meals, or anything else that fits your needs.

monday
sept 4

6
7 } → sleeping
8
9
10 ————→ biology & math class
11
12 —→ lunch w/ B   math exam
1
2
3 ————————→ study time
4
5
6
7 ————————→ club meeting
8
9

H_2O

1
2
3
4
5
6
7
8

meals

B: bagel w/ cream cheese

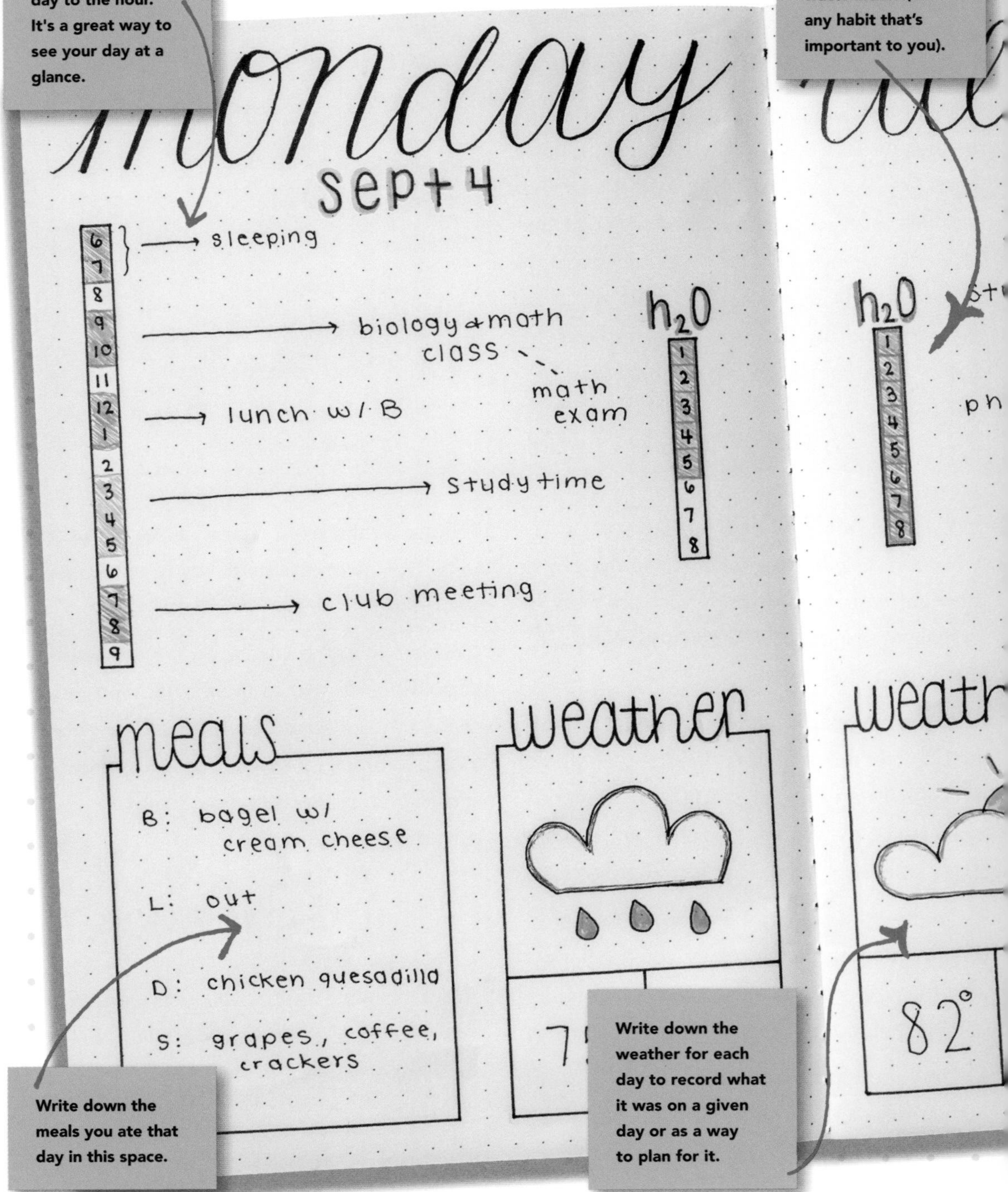

L: out

D: chicken quesadilla

S: grapes, coffee, crackers

weather

7...

tue

H_2O st...

1
2
3   ph
4
5
6
7
8

weath...

82°

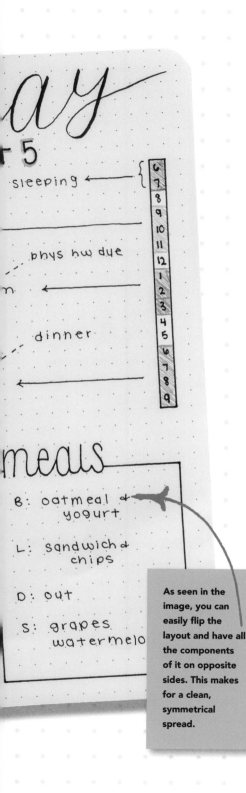

On the left-hand page image:

ay

+5

sleeping ← { 6 7 8 9 10 11 12 1 2 3 4 5 6 7 8 9

phys hw due

n ←

dinner

←

meals

B: oatmeal & yogurt

L: sandwich & chips

D: out

S: grapes watermelo

As seen in the image, you can easily flip the layout and have all the components of it on opposite sides. This makes for a clean, symmetrical spread.

Vertical Time Line with Habit Trackers

BY ASHLYN MUESER

This one-page daily layout uses a simple time line to plan your day. You can use the extra space on the page to write down what you eat, keep tabs on the weather, and track your water intake.

WHAT YOU'LL NEED

* Journal, one blank page
* Pencil and eraser
* Ruler
* Fine line black pens, 0.5 mm, 0.3 mm, and 0.1 mm
* Black brush pen
* Fine point colored markers

WHAT YOU'LL DO

1 Using the pencil, create the header on the top of the page. It should indicate the day of the week and the date.

2 Create the time line. With the pencil and a ruler, draw a narrow box on one side of the page. It should be long enough for you to write all the hours that you want to include in your schedule.

3 Create the water-intake tracker on the opposite side of the page. If you're using a dot grid paper, the number of squares in

the box should correspond to the amount of water that you want to drink each day. If your page is blank, then use your ruler and pencil to divide the box into your desired number of squares. My water-intake tracker has eight squares because I'd like to drink eight cups of water every day.

4 With the pencil, number the time line and the water-intake tracker. For the time line, write down your selected hours of the day. For the water-intake tracker, write 1–8. Feel free to use a different number range if you want to track your water intake in milliliters or another unit of measurement.

5 Using the pencil and ruler, draw two rectangles on the bottom half of the page. Divide one of the rectangles in thirds horizontally; this will be your weather box.

6 Add labels to the top of each box. To create the same labels as you see in my spread, write the words along the top edge of each box in pencil.

7 Using the pencil, outline the labels and the side and bottom edges of each box. Draw over parts of the top edge that do not intersect with your labels. For the weather box, ink the horizontal line that represents the bottom third of the rectangle. Divide this space in half vertically.

8 Draw in all the remaining lines sketched in Steps 1–4 with pen. For the header sketched in Step 1, use your black brush pen. For the remaining lines sketched in Steps 2–7, use the black 0.3 mm or 0.1 mm fine line pen. (The image shows all lines drawn using 0.3 mm pen.)

9 After waiting a few minutes for the pen to dry, erase any remaining pencil marks.

10 Add some color by using markers to write over some of your labels, like the ones for the date and the water-intake tracker.

11 Fill in the layout with your tasks and events using the 0.1 mm drawing pen. From the corresponding hour, draw an arrow or a dashed line toward the center of the page. Write down a description of your event next to the point of the arrow. Color in the corresponding times of your events on the time line with the fine point markers.

12 Throughout the day, fill in your water-intake tracker to record the number of cups of water you consumed that day.

13 To fill in the weather tracker, draw in the symbols for the particular conditions of that day in the top section of the tracker and write down the high and low temperatures in the two bottom sections.

14 In the meal diary section, note what you ate for breakfast, lunch, and dinner.

MAKE IT YOUR OWN!

Feel free to mix up the trackers and spaces to fit your daily lifestyle. You may choose to change your water-intake tracker to a calorie-intake tracker, or your meal diary to an exercise diary. Make the page work for you!

Prioritized Task Lists

BY ERIN NICHOLS

This daily layout uses a chart to categorize tasks by importance and gives you space to write down a goal to focus on. There's also room to plan your meals, note important events happening the next day, and jot down notes.

WHAT YOU'LL NEED

* Journal, one blank page
* Ruler
* Pencil and eraser
* Black fine line drawing pen
* Three colored highlighters
* Three colored fine line pens

WHAT YOU'LL DO

Draw the Priority Task List

1 Write your header at the top of the page. Make sure it includes the day of the week and the day of the month.

2 With your ruler and pencil, draw a box below your header. The box should span two-thirds of the width of the page. Leave enough space to the right of the box for the meal planner.

3 Divide the box into three equal-size columns, then go over your pencil lines with black pen and erase any remaining pencil lines.

4 Using your fine line black pen, draw a horizontal line underneath the top edge of the box to create a row for labels. Use the spaces in this row to label the columns *High*, *Medium*, and *Low*. Use the highlighters to color in the labels with different colors.

5 Fill in the Priority box with your tasks for the next day. Use a separate color for high-, medium-, and low-priority tasks. I used red for high-priority items, orange for medium-priority items, and blue for low-priority items.

Draw the Remaining Sections

6 To the right of the Priority box, draw another box the same height using your ruler and pencil.

7 Draw two horizontal lines in the box to create three equal-size rows, then go over your pencil lines with black pen and erase any remaining pencil marks.

NOTES

Monday · 6

TO-DO LIST

HIGH	MEDIUM	LOW
☑ pay utilities	☑ laundry	☑ practice letters
☑ call school	☑ unload dishes	☑ call dad
	☑ gas in car	
	☑ kid's bath	

MEALS

B	Omelet
L	Chicken Wrap
D	Turkey Lasagna

TODAY'S GOAL · Make time to read a book tonight

NOTES: download music before trip

TOMORROW: DR. APPT. @ 9am.

Tuesday · 7

HIGH	MED.	LOW
☑ DR. @ 9am	☑ Take dogs to park	☑ Go to VS
☑ Post office	☑ Bedding	☑ Nails filled
	☑ Get groceries	
	☑ Meal Prep	

MEALS

B	Pancakes
L	Cottage Cheese + Fruit
D	Leftovers

TODAY'S GOAL · Finish book in a bath and Relax.

TOMORROW:
. Lunch w/ Mom . .

Planning your meals ahead of time is a great way to save time in the evening and get a head start on any grocery shopping that you may need to do.

Use the Tomorrow section to write down asks that you didn't complete on the assigned day or to note any important upcoming events and appointments.

»»·•—→ TIP ←—•·««

If your entire daily spread doesn't fit on one page, you can certainly continue onto the next page. However, try to keep all of your tasks in the Priority box in one place.

8 With your pen, draw a small square in the upper left corner of each row and label each from top to bottom with the following abbreviations: *B* (for breakfast), *L* (for lunch), and *D* (for dinner). Label the entire box *Meals*. Fill in your meal plan, preferably during the day before so you can shop for and prepare the necessary food.

9 Switch back to your pencil and ruler. Below the Priority and Meal Planning boxes, draw a box that spans the width of the page, then go over your pencil lines with black pen and erase any remaining pencil marks. Label it *Today's Goal* with your pen.

10 In the remaining space on the page, draw two smaller boxes in pencil, each about half the width of the page, then go over your pencil lines with black pen and erase any remaining pencil marks. Label the left box *Notes* and the right box *Tomorrow* with your pen.

11 In the Notes section, write down any items on your shopping list, songs you heard, ideas you have, or anything else you want.

12 Throughout the day, add any tasks you didn't complete to the Tomorrow section. You can also use this section to add important events or appointments for the following day.

Sectioned Task List

BY EMMA BRYCE

This one-page daily layout features separate sections for tasks, appointments, notes, and anything else you want to write down. If you have a busy day, it can be useful to create a separate page for writing anything down without being restricted by the limited space in your weekly layout. The content of your daily planning pages can be different on each page. You can add additional sections as you please. For example, how about one for ideas or a shopping list?

WHAT YOU'LL NEED

* Journal, one blank page
* Pencil and eraser
* Ruler
* Fine line drawing pens in various widths
* Colored pencils

WHAT YOU'LL DO

1 Start by writing the day and date at the top of the page using your pencil. Experiment with size and different fonts. Don't be afraid to erase and start again.

2 Decide how many sections you need for your page and how big each section needs to be. Use a pencil to roughly divide the page into these sections.

3 Using your pencil, fill in the title of your first section. Continue down the page until you have labeled all of your sections.

4 Now you can start sketching your decorative elements. Stick with pencil when drafting your designs.

5 Once you are happy with the layout, use your fine line pen to outline over your pencil marks and then gently rub away your pencil marks using the eraser. Make sure the ink is dry before you start erasing

6 Color in your decorations using colored pencils and add in any final detail using fine line pens.

7 Your page is complete. Now just write down your tasks and check them off as they get done!

TUESDAY
25th july

to do

☒ wrap gift
book next appointment
food shopping

events

☒ 9:30 dentist appointment
19:30 Jessica's birthday meal

cleaning

☒ vacuum house
clean kitchen
clean bathroom

notes

· next appointment 13th June

Keep fixed appointments in order and separate them from other tasks.

You can add small drawings to each section of your daily layout, such as a pencil for Notes or a sponge and bubbles for Cleaning.

The Notes section can be useful for jotting down plans and reminders for the next day or week.

BASIC HAND-LETTERING TIPS

BY ERIN NICHOLS

Hand lettering is a great way to decorate your pages and make journaling more creative. When I started hand lettering about a year ago, my writing looked nothing like the writing I was seeing online. But because I had bought a fairly expensive set of brush pens, I was committed to learning. Every day, I would spend about fifteen to thirty minutes writing out random words. Within a few weeks I started to see my writing becoming more natural. It had a flow, and I was stoked! I've been practicing and trying new techniques since then. And even when I feel like I've perfected a technique, I find ways to improve it or change it to make it different. Hand lettering can reflect your personality and mood. It can change and be modified—and that's why I enjoy practicing and learning more about it.

Here are some tips on getting started with hand lettering and how to continue to improve your skills. I've followed this advice myself and have seen a huge difference in my hand-lettering abilities. I hope they can help you too.

* **Always start with pencil.** Before you dig out your perfect pen, grab a pencil and lightly sketch your letters out. It gives you flexibility to change how your letters look and allows you to make mistakes before you finalize your letters with a pen.
* **Try different layouts.** If you want to hand letter a quote, try adding some curves to your words or write them at an angle. To create a good curve, sketch out a half circle in pencil first. Then use your pencil to write the word along the half-circle sketch. Go over the letters with your brush marker once you are happy with how the penciled letters look.
* **Draw inspiration from everywhere.** Look at the typography on cereal boxes, movie posters, billboards, websites, and household products.
* **Make it a routine to practice your hand-lettering skill.** Whether you schedule time at night or first thing in the morning, take fifteen minutes to sit down with a pen or pencil and paper and work on your lettering. Try designing your own alphabet, writing out different words, or completing letter drills.

* **Write out pangrams.** Pangrams are a great way to practice brush lettering skills. A pangram is a phrase that uses all the letters of the alphabet, so it challenges you to work on every letter. A great starter is, "The quick brown fox jumps over the lazy dog." You can jump right in with cursive, or perfect your print letters before moving on to script.

* **Find a writing tool that works for you.** If you have been using a ballpoint pen and it doesn't feel comfortable or write smoothly enough, try using a fine line pen or a brush marker. Don't think you have to use a certain pen because someone told you to. Being comfortable with your writing instrument is important to successful lettering.

* **Don't compare your style to someone else's.** Part of what makes hand lettering so fun is that it is unique to each individual. All people have their own way of creating letters and words. And if you try to compare yourself to others, you are limiting your own creativity.

Layout with Writing Space

BY CRISTINA TAMAS

This page allows you to visualize your schedule, plan all your tasks, and write daily reflections. Its simple design offers plenty of space and flexibility for you to adapt it to any type of day that you are planning for.

WHAT YOU'LL NEED

* Journal, one blank page
* Pencil and eraser
* Ruler
* Black fine line drawing pen
* Colored markers

WHAT YOU'LL DO

1 Draw the header at the top of the page. Include the day of the week and date.

2 Under the header, use your ruler and pen to draw two horizontal lines across the page for your time tracker bar. Split this space into as many sections as you need by adding small marks on the bottom line. Write in the numbers for each hour inside each section.

3 Dedicate a section at the bottom of the page to daily journaling. Using your ruler and pen, split the page in half crosswise by drawing a vertical line across the middle. Label this space *Thoughts*. If you want to create the same label as I did, write the word first and then draw your line. Make sure your pen mark doesn't go over the label.

4 Feel free to add doodles or decorate the page however you like. You can also leave it plain.

5 The top half of the page will be used for daily tasks and notes; you can leave it blank until you start planning. Ideally, you should set up this spread the night before so that you can start filling it in the next day with a clear plan.

6 Dedicate a few minutes at the end of the day to reflect on your thoughts and write them down. Journaling is a great opportunity for you to relax and reflect on your day and to think about the things that you are grateful for or what you could improve to make the next day better.

⇒•→ TIP ←•⇐

Feel free to adapt the size of this layout depending on the type of day you're having. You don't have to dedicate half of the page to your daily planning, especially if you don't have too many tasks.

08·AUG 2017

wednesday

9 10 11 12 13 14 15 16 17 18 19 20

- DINNER WITH SARAH @ 6 PM.
- DENTIST APPOINTMENT @ 4 PM.

! ■ PREPARE DOCUMENTS FOR PRESENTATION
■ FINALIZE AND SEND REPORTS
■ CHECK & REPLY TO EMAILS
■ PAY ELECTRICITY BILL
■ DEFROST CHICKEN
→ □ MAKE GROCERY LIST FOR THIS WEEKEND
☑ FOLD LAUNDRY
- TOMORROW'S MEETING WAS CANCELLED!

thoughts

Slept really well last night. I finally woke up feeling rested - let's hope this feeling lasts! Work was okay, even though I feel like this project is never-ending and tasks keep piling up. But things should settle down next week.
Met Sarah for dinner and it was so great seeing her after what has seemed like forever! I'd forgotten how much I missed spending time with her. I should really make more time for my friends! Which reminds me, I have to shop for a gift for Tom, even though he's so hard to shop for.
Tomorrow is my first yoga class. hope I survive! ☺

70

As you finish a task, fill in the corresponding checkbox with a specific color to match it to the hourly time tracker above.

If you ever worry about wearing the same thing too often, this little box can be a lifesaver.

Write down a few sweet items of gratitude each day to add more positivity to your daily routine.

If reading matters to you, write down the book title, author, and current page to create a snapshot of your prgress every day.

Devote some space to track how much sleep and exercise you're getting each night.

june 8 fri

1 2 3 4 5 6 7 8 9 10 11 12
1 2 3 4 5 6 7 8 9 10 11 12

- [x] CALL KRISTI – FINALIZE TRIP
- [x] GROCERY SHOPPING
- [x] WEEKLY CLEAN
- [ ] SEND FINAL DRAFTS TO LINDSAY
- [x] MOVIE NIGHT – UP!

BREAKFAST	Fried Eggs & fruit
SNACK	Almonds & grapes
LUNCH	Grilled Cheese Sandwich
SNACK	Apple with Peanut Butter
DINNER	Taco Salad. Yum!
SNACK	S'mores by firepit

6:43 AM 7:37 PM 77/63

Blue Jeans, coral blouse, silver necklace, green flats.

grateful
- Home inspection went well!
- Kyle aced Vocabulary test
- Flowers from Rick ♡ XOXO
- Found plants on clearance!
- Krystal made us cookies.

| LORD BALTIMORE Stephen Doster | PAGE 209 |

| 11,739 STEPS | ELLIPTICAL 20 minutes UPPER-BODY 20 minutes | 7 HOURS |

june 9 sat

1 2 3 4 5 6 7 8 9 10 11 12
1 2 3 4 5 6 7 8 9 10 11 12

- [x] SEND FINAL DRAFTS TO LINDSAY
- [x] LAUNDRY – SHEETS & TOWELS
- [x] PARENT-TEACHER CONFERENCE
- [x] TAKE TREVOR TO AIRPORT
- [x] PACK FOR SEATTLE TRIP

BREAKFAST	Bagel with cream cheese
SNACK	String Cheese & apple
LUNCH	Leftover Taco Salad
SNACK	Chocolate Protein Shake
DINNER	Date Night! Sushi!
SNACK	Ice Cream with Rick

6:42 AM 7:38 PM 81/64

Purple polka-dot skirt, black blouse, green necklace, wedges

grateful
- Fresh bed sheets!
- Barely beating Rick at golf.
- Sticking to healthy eating
- Awesome sticker reviews!
- New suitcase for Seattle!

| LORD BALTIMORE Stephen Doster | PAGE 247 |

| 14,091 STEPS | YOGA!! AEROBICS | 6 HOURS 37 MINUTES |

Daily Planning Table

BY MICAH LEWIS

When I first began journaling, I soon discovered that I needed a hybrid way to show all of the information for my daily routine. For weeks, I worked on creating a spread that was just right for me. What resulted was a combination of journaling and planning that helps keep my life on track. The best way to make your perfect daily spread is by making a list of what matters most to you. Then decide your favorite way to make it work into your daily planning pages.

WHAT YOU'LL NEED

* Journal, one blank page
* Pencil and eraser
* Ruler
* Black fine line drawing pens in different widths
* Colored pencils
* Fine point colored markers

WHAT YOU'LL DO

1 At the top of your page, draw your favorite daily header. This can be as simple as writing the day of the week or recording the month, date, and day of the week in a pretty banner.

2 Underneath your header, draw a small rectangle using your ruler and pencil to create a table for your twenty-four–hour time bar. Divide the rectangle in half crosswise. To create twenty-four equal-size spaces, draw eleven vertical lines inside the rectangle. Write the numbers 1–12 on each row of the rectangle.

3 Using a pencil, draw a long rectangle that spans the length of the page below the time bar. Divide the rectangle into the sections

⟫⟶ TIP ⟵⟪

Modify any section to track other hobbies or routines that are important to you. Did you reach the next level in your video game? Did you walk your dog today? Where did your evening run take you? Journaling is all about tracking what matters most to you!

depicted in the photo or create your own sections and spaces that suit your daily routine.

4 With your pen, outline the pencil lines. Write or draw a doodle inside each box to label in each section.

5 Repeat this spread to create a page for each day of the week. Depending on your design, you might be able to fit more than one Daily Spread per page. You'll draw better and faster with practice, so don't worry about the time it takes when you're first starting out.

6 Use colored pencils and fine-tip markers to add color, detail, and dimension to your spread. Because most of my writing is in black ink, I love how adding color to doodles makes the pages come to life.

7 After your spread is set, fill in the details of your day. You can add items throughout the day as they happen, or complete it all at once each evening. You can also fill out your upcoming tasks for the next day so that you hit the ground running when you wake up.

»•→ TIP ←•«

It can take weeks to get the perfect daily spread for your lifestyle. Don't be afraid to makes changes and delete boxes that aren't working for you! Tweaking helps you get it just right for you.

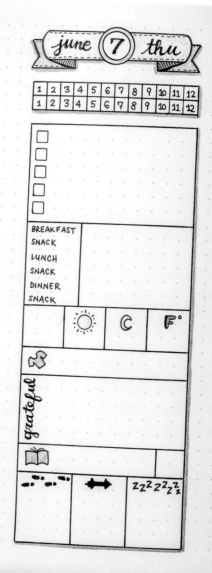

Workout Tracker with Fitness Diary

BY MARIETHERES VIEHLER

I recently joined a gym, and I was looking for a spread to track all the different fitness classes I wanted to take. I'm not a big fan of detailed fitness layouts as I tend to lose the motivation to write everything down after a few days, but it helps to have a page where I can track what kind of workout I've done on a specific day. It's very rewarding to look back at this spread at the end of the month and see how much I've done for my body during the last few weeks.

WHAT YOU'LL NEED

* Journal, one blank two-page spread
* Pencil and eraser
* Ruler
* Black gel pen
* Colored pens

WHAT YOU'LL DO

1 With your pen, create a header on the left page. It can be minimal or more decorative—it's totally up to you and how much time you want to spend setting up the spread.

2 Below your header, write down the days of the week using your pen. With your pencil and ruler, draw boxes for each day of the month to create a calendar. I like to leave a little space between each box.

3 With your pen, outline the boxes. To save time, you can just outline the corners of each box instead of the entire edge. Number each box with the date.

4 Create a color-coding scheme. Each color describes a fitness class or workout. With your colored pens, make a simple legend below your calendar that explains what each color means.

5 Erase all the extra pencil marks. Make sure to let the ink on the page dry to avoid any smudging!

6 To use your calendar tracker, fill in the box that corresponds to the date that you went to a class or completed a workout.

7 The right page functions as a fitness diary. You can use it to write a simple list of workouts like I did or as a very detailed diary. It doesn't need to be very neat and orderly; remember, it's there to help you with your fitness journey.

MAKE IT YOUR OWN!

You can turn this spread into a monthly planning page. The color coding is perfect for categorizing all your different appointments and tasks. You can use the right page for writing notes or goals.

workout t[

M   T   W

2	3	4
9	10	11
16	17	18
23	24	25
60	31	

Yoga
Pilates
Ballet
Swimming

The colors give a better overview and make it easy to distinguish between the different classes instantly.

Use the calendar to track your attendance to your fitness classes and practice sessions.

S   S

7   8

14   15

21   22

28   29

1 S   Swimming: 10 x 50m, 1 x 400m freestyle,
                     4 x 100 medley, 4 x 25m speed

4 W   Swimming: 600m warmup, 10 x 100m freestyle,
                     12 x 25m medley, 100m cooldown

6 F   Pilates: Wake up + connect workout

10 T   Swimming: 10 x 50m, 1 x 300m freestyle,
                     4 x 100 medley, 2 x 25 speed

13 F   Yoga: Body Flow for the first time

14 S   Ballet: Exhausted (too much)

15 S   Swimming: 600m warmup, 10 x 100m freestyle,
                     12 x 25m medley, 100m cooldown

18 W   Swimming: 10 x 50m, 1 x 400m freestyle,
                     4 x 100 medley, 4 x 25m speed

20 F   Pilates: Better sleep routine

24 T   Swimming: 600m warmup, 10 x 100m freestyle,
                     12 x 25m medley, 100m cooldown

29 S   Swimming: 10 x 50m, 1 x 400 freestyle,
                     4 x 100m medley, 4 x 25m speed

A fitness diary is the perfect space to keep notes for each workout or class. I can see how my times improve or note how I'm feeling when I exercise.

Daily Wellness Tracker

BY ERIN NICHOLS

Keep track of your sleep, energy, and mood with this spread. With a line graph, you can see how each aspect of your life affects the other, or if there is any association at all. There's also space for a very brief description of events that might affect any of the three things you're tracking.

WHAT YOU'LL NEED

* Journal, one blank page
* Pencil and eraser
* Ruler
* Black fine line pen
* Three fine line colored pens

WHAT YOU'LL DO

1 Orient your page horizontally. Use your black pen and ruler to draw a large box. It should be large enough to create a graph that has a vertical axis with ten marks for your ratings and a horizontal axis with a mark for each day of the month.

2 Label the vertical axis by writing in the numbers 1–10 along the left edge of the rectangle. Repeat for the right edge.

3 Label the horizontal axis by writing in the days of the month along the bottom edge of the rectangle.

4 In the space around your graph, draw your *Daily Tracker* header. I chose to place *Daily* on the left of the graph and *Header* on the right of the graph.

5 To create a small legend to indicate which colors represent sleep, energy, and mood, draw a narrow rectangle below the graph. Place the label on the left side of the rectangle. Draw three smaller boxes inside the rectangle. Label each small box with the item you're tracking, and fill in the boxes with the colored pens. Use a different color for each item.

6 Just below the legend, draw a horizontal line all the way across the page. Add the label *Daily Notes* anywhere above your line.

7 With your pencil and ruler, divide the space below the horizontal line into three columns. Using your pencil lines as a guide, write the days of the month in three columns. You should have about ten days per column. Erase the pencil lines after you've written all the days.

8 To fill in the line graph, mark dots within the box to note how many hours of sleep you got, and rate your energy levels and mood for the given day. On the following day do the same, and then use your ruler to connect the dots from the previous day to the dot for your current day. Don't forget to add a few words to the Daily Notes section.

MAKE IT YOUR OWN!

You can turn this wellness tracker into an exercise tracker. Instead of recording the quality of your sleep, your mood, or energy level, you can record how many steps you've taken or minutes you've spent exercising. In the Notes section, write down the details of your workout and how you felt afterward.

»»•—→ **TIP** ←—•««

After you have spent at least a week filling in this spread, look at how your sleep affects your mood and energy levels. Then, you can adjust your sleep schedule if needed. Oftentimes, when I've only slept for four or five hours, my energy and mood levels suffer the following day, which gives me insight into how much sleep I need to be getting to have a good day.

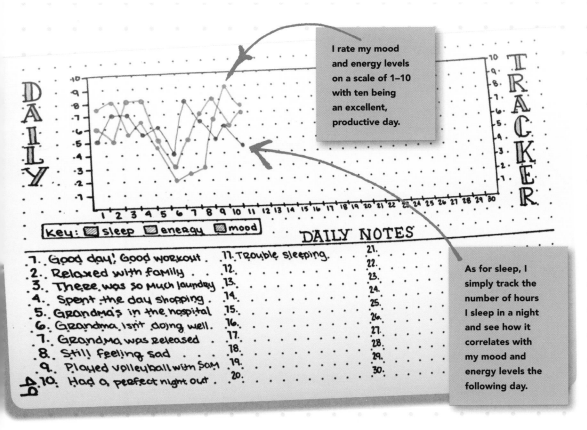

I rate my mood and energy levels on a scale of 1–10 with ten being an excellent, productive day.

As for sleep, I simply track the number of hours I sleep in a night and see how it correlates with my mood and energy levels the following day.

Key: ▨ sleep ▨ energy ▨ mood

DAILY NOTES

1. Good day! Good workout.
2. Relaxed with family.
3. There was so much laundry
4. Spent the day shopping.
5. Grandma's in the hospital
6. Grandma isn't doing well.
7. Grandma was released
8. Still feeling sad
9. Played volleyball with Sam
10. Had a perfect night out.
11. Trouble sleeping.
12.
13.
14.
15.
16.
17.
18.
19.
20.
21.
22.
23.
24.
25.
26.
27.
28.
29.
30.

sept 4-10

tr

water

8
7
6
5
4
3
2
1

m t w r f s s

calories

2k

1k

m t w r f s s

symb

ru
su
bi

miles

10
9
8
7
6
5
4
3
2
1

other habits

	m	t	w	r	f	s	s
log meals	■	■	□	■	□	□	■
breakfast	■	■	■	■	■	■	■
veggies	■	■	■	□	■	■	■
fruit	■	■	■	■	■	■	□
vitamins	■	■	■	■	■	■	■
min carbs	■	■	■	■	□	□	■

trainir

yoga

pilate

The symbols are compiled in a directory so that you can easily reference the type of exercise that you recorded in the bar graph below it.

ker

elliptical

walking

This bar graph on the right page tracks the number of miles exercised with various methods.

r f S S

ses

t w r f S S

This table tracks class attendance and training sessions.

Weekly Exercise and Diet Tracker

BY ASHLYN MUESER

This weekly tracker is designed for the health-focused individual. There are areas to track both diet- and exercise-related items, along with trackers that are set up with graphs to give you a visual summary of what you did in a week.

WHAT YOU'LL NEED

* Journal, one blank two-page spread
* Pencil and eraser
* Ruler
* Black fine line pens, 0.5 mm, 0.3 mm, and 0.1 mm
* Colored markers

WHAT YOU'LL DO

Draw Your Headers

1 Using the pencil, sketch the headers on the top of each page. For the left page, write the month and the dates for the week that you're tracking. For the right page, you can just write *Tracker*.

Draw Your Water- and Caloric-Intake Trackers

2 With the pencil and a ruler, trace the outlines for your water and caloric intake trackers on the left page. Split the top section of the page in half vertically. On the left half, draw your horizontal and vertical axes. If your page has a printed grid, you can use the grid pattern to divide your axis. If your page is blank, then use your ruler and pencil to draw a box and trace a grid inside the box. Your horizontal axis will take up eight squares on the grid (one square for each day of the week and one extra on the left so that your horizontal line intersects with the vertical axis). Your vertical axis will take up nine squares (eight are for the cups of water to drink and the extra on the bottom for your axes to intersect). Copy the same horizontal and vertical axes to the right side of the page.

3 Divide the axes of each habit tracker. For the Water-Intake tracker, number each square on your vertical axis 1–8. For the Caloric Intake tracker, mark your vertical axis in 1,000-calorie increments with the top of the axis denoting the maximum calories to consume that day (the image shows tracking for 2,000 calories with each square representing 250 calories). Write down the abbreviations of each day of the week for the horizontal axes of both bar graphs.

4 Label each tracker using any extra space to the left or above the bar graphs.

Draw Your Other-Habits Tracker

5 In the space below your Water- and Caloric-Intake trackers, draw your header for your Other-Habits tracker. Create a grid beneath the header, if needed.

6 With your pencil and ruler, draw a horizontal line below your header. The line should be at least sixteen squares long. Each day of the week will take up one square with one buffer square surrounding it. The remaining squares will provide space to write down your habits.

7 Draw a vertical line that intersects this horizontal line to finish your two-column table, making sure to leave some space between the start of the horizontal line and the intersection of the two lines.

8 In the left column, list the habits that you want to track. Write in one habit per row.

9 In the right column, use your colored markers to draw seven boxes in each row of the table underneath the days of the week. Leave one square's worth of space around each side of the colored boxes. Feel free to color the boxes as you desire. I chose to use

one color for each habit, but you could fill in a color for each day of the week or make the colors completely random.

Draw Your Miles and Classes Tracker

10 On the right page, outline a box below the header with the pencil and a ruler. This will be the symbol directory for your graph.

11 Divide the space below the legend evenly. In the top space, draw the horizontal and vertical axes for the mile tracker bar graph. The horizontal axis has sixteen squares, one for each day of the week and a buffer square on either side of each day's bar. The vertical axis is twelve squares tall, one square for each day of the week and two extra squares on the bottom to allow the line to intersect with the horizontal axis. Number each box in the vertical axis 1–10.

12 In the bottom space, draw another table for the class attendance tracker.

13 With the 0.3 mm black pen, label each tracker and the horizontal and vertical axes on the graphs. Fill in the symbol directory with the exercise categories you're tracking and their corresponding colors.

14 Trace the pencil outlines of each tracker using a 0.3 mm black pen. After waiting a few minutes for the ink to dry, erase any pencil marks.

15 Fill in the trackers throughout the week using the colored markers. The Water- and Calorie-Intake trackers are best filled out throughout the day so that they help you stay accountable and on your healthy diet. The remaining trackers can all be filled out at the end of the day.

HEALTH AND WELLNESS

Food Diary Spread

BY CRISTINA TAMAS

This simple spread helps you build healthy habits and become more conscious about your food choices. The calendar-style layout makes it easy for you to stay on track and fill in the sections for each day.

WHAT YOU'LL NEED

* Journal, one blank two-page spread
* Pencil and eraser
* Ruler
* Black fine line drawing pen
* Colored markers and pencils

WHAT YOU'LL DO

1 With your pencil and ruler, divide each page into four columns and as many rows as the number of weeks in the month.

2 Draw the calendar using the pencil marks as a guide. With a pen, add the dates at the top of each box. Outline the spaces with dates inside. When the ink is dry, erase any remaining pencil marks.

3 Using a marker, draw a thick line across the top of each row for a bit of decoration.

4 Using your pen, add the page title in any space you have on the spread.

5 Draw the Healthy Habits tracker in the last column on the right page. Using your ruler and pen, draw a vertical line. You should have one row for each day of the month. Starting from the top of the vertical line, draw a short horizontal line for your habit icons, making sure you have one column for each habit.

6 Write the days of the month in the space to the left of the vertical line. On top of the horizontal line, draw the icons representing each habit and the label.

7 To fill in this spread, write down in each space of the calendar what you've eaten. For the Healthy Habits tracker, add a large dot into the space that corresponds to the applicable habit and day of the week.

MAKE IT YOUR OWN!

* Instead of using this calendar layout for tracking food intake, you can use the space to write down information about your workouts, water-intake, or any other health- and fitness-related habits.

* This practical layout is a great variation of the Calendar-Style Layout (page 29) and can be used for planning your months.

food & health

4	5	6	7
B: SANDWICH L: ENCHILADAS D: FISH + POTATOES S: FROZEN YOGHURT	B: WAFFELS L: CHEESE PIZZA D: — S: PEANUTS, APPLE ICE CREAM	B: FRENCH TOAST L: VEGGIE WRAP D: BLACK BEAN SOUP S: APPLE CHIPS	B: CEREAL L: VEGGIE ROLLS D: CHICKEN SOUP S: —
11	**12**	**13**	**14**
B: EGGS + BACON L: TUNA SANDWICH D: VEGGIES S: WATERMELON	B: SANDWICH L: VEGGIE WRAP D: CHICKEN PARM S: CARROTS	B: PANCAKES L: CHICKEN PARM D: LEFTOVERS S: CHOCOLATE	B: — L: CHICKEN SALAD D: STEAK + POTATOES S: —
18	**19**	**20**	**21**
B: TOAST + JAM L: — D: SALMON + RICE S: DONUT SMOOTHIE	B: — L: LEFTOVERS D: TUNA SANDWICH S: CHOCOLATE HUMMUS	B: SANDWICH L: ENCHILADAS D: TAPAS SALAD S: —	B: CEREAL L: GUACAMOLE D: PESTO PASTA S: —
25	**26**	**27**	**28**
B: CASSEROLE	B: PANCAKES ... POTATOES ...L	B: APPLES L: CHICKEN WRAP D: LEFTOVERS S: CAKE	B: SMOOTHIE L: CHINESE FOOD D: — S: DONUT

1	2	3
B: CEREAL L: HASH BROWNS D: CHICKEN SALAD S: WATERMELON	B: FRENCH TOAST L: SALMON + RICE D: HUMMUS S: MUFFINS	B: GRANOLA BAR L: TURKEY SANDWICH D: TACOS S: APPLE CHIPS ICE CREAM
8	**9**	**10**
B: TOAST + AVOCADO L: GUACAMOLE D: KALE SALAD S: PEANUTS	B: BANANAS L: VEGGIE SOUP D: GREEN JUICE S: DARK CHOCOLATE	B: SANDWICH L: PASTA D: MEATBALLS S: HUMMUS BABY CARROTS
15	**16**	**17**
B: FRUIT L: STUFFED PEPPERS D: PULLED PORK SAND. S: MUFFINS CRAKERS	B: GRANOLA BAR L: KALE SALAD D: GREEN JUICE S: CHOCOLATE	B: — L: ENCHILADAS D: SALAD WRAP S: NACHOS
22	**23**	**24**
B: SANDWICH L: NOODLES D: BLACK BEAN SOUP S: —	B: PANCAKES L: VEGGIE SOUP D: PASTA S: —	B: EGGS + TOAST L: TUNA SANDWICH D: SMOOTHIE S: BANANAS
29	**30**	**31**
B: — L: CAESAR SALAD D: MAC & CHEESE S: HUMMUS BABY CARROTS		...ES

healthy habits

🍽️ 🥤 🕐 H 🧘 🏋️

1
2
3
4
5
6
7
8
9
10
11
12
13
14
15
16
17
18
19
20
21
22
23
24
25
26
27
28
29
30
31

habit tracker

These mini icons represent the habits you want to track. You can track as few or as many habits as you want.

Mark your boxes with small diagonal lines to create a nice design.

The legend reminds you what each icon in your habit tracker represents.

F 1
S 2
S 3
M 4
T 5
W 6
T 7
F 8
S 9
S 10
M 11
T 12
W 13
T 14
F 15
S 16
S 17
M 18
T 19
W 20
T 21
F 22
S 23
S 24
M 25
T 26
W 27
T 28
F 29
S 30

Legend:
- workout
- clean house
- bed by 11
- ate at home
- ate healthy
- 10k+ steps

48

Icon Habit Tracker

BY ERIN NICHOLS

Become more aware of what you are doing on a daily basis with this habit tracker. Fill in a square every time you complete a task and see exactly how your habits match up with your goals.

WHAT YOU'LL NEED

* Journal, one blank page
* Pencil and eraser
* Ruler
* Black fine line pen
* Pastel highlighter

WHAT YOU'LL DO

1 Leaving room for a header at the top of the page, use your black pen to number the days of the month down the left side of your page.

2 Next to the numbers, write the first letter of the corresponding days of the week. Then use your ruler and pencil to create a box around the letters and numbers.

3 To create the rest of the tracker, draw a larger box next to the one with the letters and numbers. The two boxes will share a vertical edge.

4 Create the individual spaces you will use to track your habits. If your page has a printed grid, you can use the grid pattern to divide your tracker into individual squares. Each habit will have one square for each day. If your page is blank, then use your ruler and pencil to measure how large each square should be and trace a grid inside the box.

5 Just above where you wrote the days of the month, start drawing the icons representing your habits in a horizontal row.

6 Draw your header. To re-create the one on this page, write the month in large letters with your highlighter. With your black pen, write *Habit Tracker* on top of the month.

7 To the right of the grid, draw a small box with your pen and ruler for your legend. Make sure your box has enough room to fit all of your icons.

8 Inside the box, redraw your icons and label them with the habits they stand for. Then label the box, if you like.

9 Draw lines through the boxes that match the habits you completed at the end of your day or the first thing the next morning, so you don't forget what you have done. For habits you did not complete, leave the box blank.

Monthly Time Tracker

BY MARIETHERES VIEHLER

As someone who is self-employed, my time is on the top of my mind. To see where it's going, I use this Time Tracker spread with color-coding. I prefer to keep this layout simple so I can quickly fill it out each day and at the end of the month easily see how I've spent my time.

WHAT YOU'LL NEED

* Journal, one blank two-page spread
* Pencil and eraser
* Ruler
* Black gel pen
* Colored pens

WHAT YOU'LL DO

1 Start with the header. Use your pen to write *Time Tracker* across the top of the left page. You can include the month in your header, if you like. I usually keep it pretty simple to save some time.

2 With your pen, write the days of the month down the left side of each page. Leave a space between each day. You can add the days of the week as well to get a better overview of the way you spend your time, especially if your schedule on the weekdays is very different from on the weekends.

3 At the top of each page (below your header), write down the hours of the day. The number of hours you can fit on each page will vary from notebook to notebook. Because I use an A6 size journal, my record of events tends to be shorter, but I always try to fit in the hours between 7:00 a.m. and 1:00 a.m.

4 Separate the daytime and nighttime hours by drawing boxes in each row of your time tracker. I like to use a typical workday as the "daytime" hours, but how you choose to separate your day always depends on your personal schedule.

5 Because this tracker is color-coded, create a small legend on top of the right page. Use a different color for each item that you want to track.

6 Erase all the extra pencil marks. Make sure to let the ink on the page dry to avoid any smudging!

7 After setting the tracker up, record how you spend your time every day by filling in the corresponding part of the boxes with the color you assigned to the task. I try to do this immediately after waking up or after a task is done, so I don't forget.

By dividing the hours into day and night, I get a better overview when I record my time. It especially helps me see if I sleep enough and if I've kept to my bedtime.

The hours that you track can always vary depending on your individual lifestyle.

time tracker

Color coding gives a clear view of the different categories and makes it easy to see where the time went at the end of the month.

//// Fitness   //// Sleep   //// Work

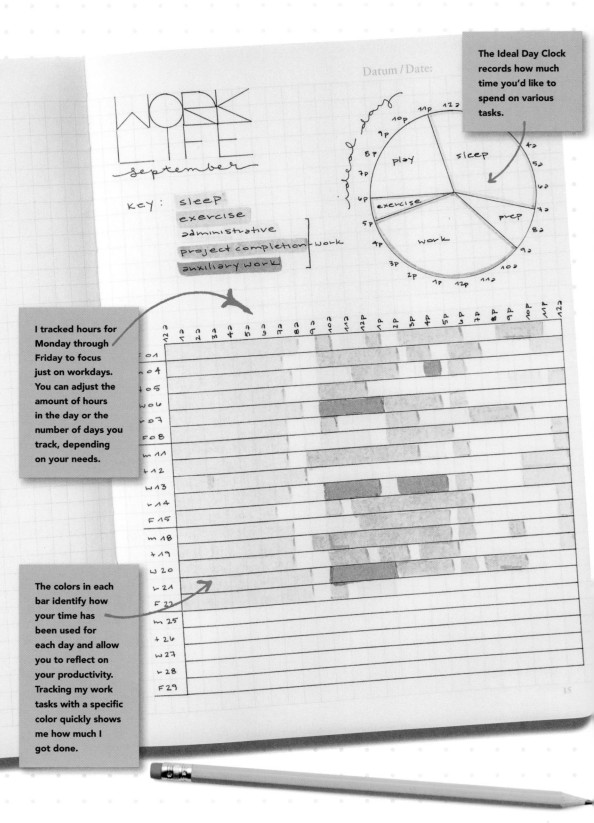

Datum / Date:

WORK
LIFE
september

key: sleep
exercise
administrative
project completion-work
auxiliary work

The Ideal Day Clock records how much time you'd like to spend on various tasks.

ideal day

10p 11p 12a
9p
8p   play   sleep   4a
7p   5a
6p   6a
     exercise   7a
5p   prep   8a
4p   work   9a
3p   10a
  2p 1p 12p 11a

I tracked hours for Monday through Friday to focus just on workdays. You can adjust the amount of hours in the day or the number of days you track, depending on your needs.

The colors in each bar identify how your time has been used for each day and allow you to reflect on your productivity. Tracking my work tasks with a specific color quickly shows me how much I got done.

15

WORK AND PRODUCTIVITY

Weekly Time Tracker

BY CINDY THOMPSON

When working from home or with a very flexible schedule, it can be tricky to know exactly how much time you are putting toward various tasks. I've used this time tracker to help me identify how much time I spend on work on a weekly basis and measure my productivity against an ideal day. The great thing about this layout is its versatility. You can include as much or as little detail as you'd like.

WHAT YOU'LL NEED

* Journal, one blank page
* Pencil and eraser
* Ruler
* Circle stencil
* Black fine line pen, 0.05 mm
* Color brush pens or markers
* Protractor (optional)

WHAT YOU'LL DO

1 On the top left corner of the page, create a header using the black pen.

2 At the top right of the page, draw a circle for the Ideal Day Clock using the black pen, ruler, and circle stencil.

3 Using the protractor and pencil, lightly sketch small dashes along the edge of the circle that correspond with the hours on your clock. Mark the center of the circle as well. For a twenty-four–hour clock, as shown in this layout, the hours are 15 degrees apart. You can also do this freehand if you do not have a protractor.

4 With the pencil marks as a guide, add the hours along the outside of the clock with the black pen.

5 Using the ruler and black pen, draw lines to separate the clock into the different segments of your day. Each line should start at a pencil dash and end at the center point.

6 Once all the lines are drawn, gently use the eraser to erase the pencil dashes. Label the segments using the black pen.

7 Create the time line by drawing a box that fills the bottom half of the page using the black pen and ruler. The number of rows in the box should match the number of days you want to track. The right edge of box should meet the margin of your page, but leave some extra space next to the left edge of the box for labels.

8 Divide the box into equal-size rows by drawing horizontal lines inside the box with your pencil and ruler. On my page, I extended some of the lines outside the box to separate each workweek.

9 Using the black pen, write the days of the month and week along the left edge of the box and the hours of the day along the top of the box.

10 In the extra space between the header and the time line, write down the types of tasks that you're tracking. Color-code the different categories using colored brush pens or markers. Use these colors to outline the corresponding clock segments as well.

11 Throughout the day, fill in the bars with your chosen colors. Sometimes, it will be easy to do so as soon as you are done with a task, such as when you are working at your desk. Other times, you'll have to go back in at the end of the day to add things, like exercising, that may have happened while you didn't have your journal with you.

MAKE IT YOUR OWN!

It's easy to add and subtract items from this tracker. You could keep tabs on errands, hobbies, or your work schedule to keep a very complete view of your day, or you could just focus on one of these items. Students can use this layout as a study tracker and mark off the times you study or work on homework for each class.

⇝•→ TIPS ←•⇜

* To color-code a variety of tasks that fall under the same category, use different shades of the same color to help break down what type of tasks were worked on. In my layout, I used different shades of blue to organize my work-related items.

* You can make the time line more focused by tracking fewer hours and breaking each hour into fifteen or thirty-minute segments. This could be great for tracking a five-hour study session, for example. You can use different colors to represent different subjects.

* Instead of writing the time of day at the top of the time line, you can simply number the spaces. This creates a time line that tracks the total hours spent on a task without needing to record what part of the day the task took place.

Sleep and Productivity Tracker

BY CRISTINA TAMAS

This spread helps you track your daily sleeping patterns and time management. It allows you to collect data about the possible correlation between the quality and quantity of your sleep and your productivity levels. Together, the spreads make a complete visual representation of your day: how many hours you've slept, how many you've spent being productive, and what type of activities you've engaged in.

WHAT YOU'LL NEED

* ✳ Journal, one blank two-page spread
* ✳ Pencil and eraser
* ✳ Black fine line drawing pen or any pen of your choice
* ✳ Colored markers and pencils
* ✳ Ruler (optional)

WHAT YOU'LL DO

1 On the top of each page, write the title of each tracker. I wrote *Sleep* on the left page and *Productivity* on the right page.

2 For both trackers, write the days of the month and the corresponding weekday abbreviations, starting from the bottom left side of each page. With your pen and ruler, draw a vertical line next to each column of days to separate them from the boxes that you'll fill in. For the Sleep Tracker, write the hours in the day and a scale for the quality of the sleep across the top of the left page. With your pen and ruler, draw a vertical line down the page to divide the hours and quality of sleep sections. Adding the hours at the top of the Productivity Tracker isn't necessary; this tracker is meant to provide you with a quick overview of how much time you've spent on certain activities each day in total rather than indicate the exact hour the activity took to complete.

3 With your pen and ruler, draw a vertical line on the right of your Productivity Tracker for a Review section. Divide the column into three sections with two horizontal lines. The top section should be twice as large as the other two. At the top of the column, write *Review*.

4 In the bottom section of the column, create the color-coded legend. Decide which activities you'd like to track (i.e., work, running errands, doing fun or relaxing activities, etc.). Assign a color to each.

5 If your page has a printed grid, use the grid pattern to divide the Sleep Tracker and Productivity Tracker into individual squares. If your journal has blank pages, then use your ruler and pencil to measure how large each square should be and trace a grid inside both trackers. To fill in your trackers, color in the squares based on how many hours you spent on your different activities. For the line graph section in the Sleep Tracker, plot the point that corresponds to your sleep quality rating and the date. With you ruler, connect the point to the one that you added the previous day.

6 At the end of the month, fill in the Review section. Count how many hours you've spent on each category and write them down. Adding up all these hours will give you the total amount of hours. To create the pie chart, find out what percentage each category represents of the total, and split the circle accordingly. You don't have to use precise numbers—an estimate is good enough.

»•→ TIP ←•«

You can join these two trackers by writing all twenty-four hours of the day at the top and tracking both sleep and productivity on the same row. If the space allows, you can also add the sleep-quality tracker and Review section at the end of your combined tracker.

Track the times you go to sleep and when you wake up every day. The numbers at the top of the tracker list the hours in a day (from 9:00 p.m. to 10:00 a.m., in this case).

SLEEP

9 10 11 12 1 2 3 4 5 6 7 8

T 1
W 2
T 3
F 4
S 5
S 6
M 7
T 8
W 9
T 10
F 11
S 12
S 13
M 14
T 15
W 16
T 17
F 18
S 19
S 20
M 21
T 22
W 23
T 24
F 25
S 26
S 27
M 28
T 29
W 30

PRODUCTIVITY

REVIEW

Fill in this section at the end of the month with the data that you gather from the trackers. This refers to the general Review section (including the sleep stats).

1
2
3
4
5
6
7
8
9
10
11
12
13
14
15
16
17
18
19
20
21
22
23
24
25
26
27
28

WORK: 180h
ERRANDS: 41h
APPT: 14h
FUN: 48h
HOBBIES: 26h

☾ AVG. ASLEEP: 11:30 pm
☼ AVG. AWAKE: 6:45 am
Zᶻ AVG. HOURS / DAY: 7.5h
★ AVG. QUALITY: 3.3 / 5

WORK / BUSINESS
HOUSEWORK / ERRANDS
MEETINGS / APPOINTMENTS
GOING OUT / FUN
HOBBIES / CRAFTS

61

You can use this section to rate the quality of your sleep. The line graph is a great visual representation for identifying your sleep patterns and what influences them.

Track how much time you spend on certain areas of each day. Each square represents a unit of time, such as one hour.

You can create a color-code for these squares based on the type of activities that take up your time.

Goal Tracker

BY ASHLYN MUESER

This spread allows you to list three of your biggest goals for the year, note how you will accomplish those goals, and track your progress. Rather than simply listing your goals, this layout helps you define the steps needed to accomplish each one and keep you accountable throughout the year as you reflect on your accomplishments or challenges.

WHAT YOU'LL NEED

* Journal, one blank two-page spread
* Pencil and eraser
* Ruler
* Black fine line drawing pens, 0.5 mm, 0.3 mm, and 0.1 mm
* Colored markers

WHAT YOU'LL DO

Make the Goal-Description Page

1 Using the pencil, sketch the header on the top of the left page. You can customize your header to reflect your personal style.

2 With the pencil and ruler, draw three equal-size rectangles below the header. Leave some extra space to the left of each box for labels. Trace the pencil outlines of each box using a 0.3 mm black pen. After the ink dries, erase any pencil marks.

3 Label each box with the 0.3 mm pen with *Goal #1*, *Goal #2*, and *Goal #3*. For a clean look, orient the labels vertically.

4 In the top of each box, write your goal and how you plan to achieve it. You can add some color by highlighting the goals in each box with the markers.

Make the Checking-In Table

5 Orient the right page horizontally. Using the black 0.5 mm pen, write *Checking In* on the top left of the page.

6 Sketch the outline of the checking-in table. With the pencil and ruler, draw a large box below the header. The box should take up the remaining space on the page.

7 Create five rows by drawing four horizontal lines inside the box. You will need less space in the first row because you will only use it to label the columns.

8 Fill in the first box in the first row with diagonal lines. In the remaining boxes in the first row, color in the boxes with the corresponding color for each goal. Label the columns *Goal #1*, *Goal #2*, and *Goal #3* with the 0.3 mm black drawing pen.

9 Trace the pencil outlines of each tracker using a 0.3 mm black pen. After the ink dries, erase any pencil marks.

10 Record notes about your progress at the designated check-in times.

MAKE IT YOUR OWN!

If you would like to track more than three goals, you can always make two copies of these pages in your journal, or you can decrease the size for each section to make room for an additional goal. Just be sure to not spread yourself too thin, and be realistic with the number and scope of your goals to give yourself the best chance at achieving them!

Describe your goals and your plan for accomplishing them in the boxes on the left page.

You can color-code each goal to make the description and check-in page more cohesive.

The tracker on the right page gives you room to note your progress on each goal throughout the year.

2017 goals

goal #1

- lose 20 lbs.

accomplish by:
- exercising 4x/week
- logging food 6x/week + eating mindfully

goal #2

- pass all classes w/ B or higher

accomplish by:
- complete all assignments
- start studying for exams at least 1 week beforehand

goal #3

- have a more positive attitude

accomplish by:
- go to yoga at least 2x/week
- do things that make me happy regularly (like journaling)

checking-in

	goal #1	goal #2	goal #3
march	lost 5 lbs - get better w/ diet	good start! - plan studying better	mostly positive - do more yoga
june	total loss: 10 lbs - struggling w/ diet log	Got all B+ + up! - do the same next semester	a little down - enjoy more "me" time
sept	total loss: 12 lbs - get back into exercise	rough start - make better study plans	better! - continue w/ what I'm doi[ng]
1 year			

semester o

schedule

	m	t	w	n	f
8					
9	math		math		math
10		bio		bio	
11					
12					
1		physics	chem lab	physics lab	chem
2					
3	chem				
4					
5					

In this box, you can lay out your weekly course schedule.

Use color-coding to categorize the information on the schedule by class.

course info

math
Dr. Williams
willams@school.edu
- HW every week
- 3 exams + final

chem
Dr. Johnson
johnson@school.edu
- Labs + HW every week
- 3 exams + final

bio
Dr. Smith
smith@school.edu
- 6 reports, 4 HWs
- 2 exams + final

physics
Dr. James
james@school.edu
- Labs every week
- 1 midterm, 1 final

Write down any course info you find important. Here, I've noted the names and email addresses of my professors, along with the number of important assignments and exams.

8

aug

sept

oct

n
o
v

rview

Write important dates during each month of the semester here.

tarts - 21

rt - 31

ay: no class - 4
exam 1 - 13

exam 1 - 14
ort + HW - 21 + exam 1

s: exam midterm - 5
ort + HW - 10
exam 2 - 20
exam 2 - 27
ort - 31

port + HW - 14 + exam 2

exam 3 - 13
exam 3 - 17
ksgiving: no class - 19-25

eport + HW - 5
cs: final exam - 12
: final exam - 12
: final exam - 13
final exam - 15

9

14   15

WORK AND PRODUCTIVITY

Semester Overview

BY ASHLYN MUESER

This spread is a place to note your class schedule, course information, and important dates. The left page offers a great overview of your classes, while the right is helpful for keeping all the important dates, such as exams or paper deadlines, all in one place.

WHAT YOU'LL NEED

* Journal, one blank two-page spread
* Pencil and eraser
* Ruler
* Black fine line drawing pens, 0.5 mm, 0.3 mm, and 0.1 mm
* Colored markers

WHAT YOU'LL DO

1 Using the pencil, sketch in the header at the top of the spread.

2 With the pencil and ruler, draw two equal-size boxes that span the width of the page below the header on the left page. On the right page, draw one large box.

3 Label each box with the 0.3 mm black drawing pen as shown in the photo. Place the labels at the top edge of the boxes.

4 Inside the Schedule box, draw a smaller rectangle. Draw a horizontal line near the top edge of the rectangle and a vertical line near the left edge of the rectangle. Draw four more vertical lines to divide the space to the right of the first line into five even sections. Fill in the cells in the top row with the days of the workweek. In the leftmost column, write the hours of the day that you want to schedule.

5 Outline the header and the edges of the boxes with the 0.3 mm pen, allowing the inked edges to touch the labels, if you prefer. For the table in the Schedule box, you can leave the top and left outlines of the top left cell in pencil. When the ink dries, erase any pencil marks.

6 To fill in your class schedule, draw a colored rectangle to indicate the day, time, and length of each class. Write the class name in each colored rectangle with the 0.3 mm black drawing pen.

7 In the Course Info box, fill in information and dates for your classes using the 0.1 mm black drawing pen. To make the most of your available space, organize your text into two columns. You can underline the course titles in the Course Info section using the colors that you used for your class schedule.

8 On the right page, add equally spaced and sized brackets next to months. For months where school is in session for a shorter amount of time, like August in my page, you can create a bracket that has one less row than the rest of the months. Write down your important assignments, due dates, and exams for each month. Color-code the assignments by drawing dots next to each description using your colored markers.

Savings and Debt Tracker

BY CINDY THOMPSON

Tracking your finances can be a challenge, especially if you are managing different accounts with different goals in mind. This two-page spread allowed me to keep all my savings- and student loan–related transactions in one place. It also gave me a visual indicator of how much progress I was making toward my goals. Because I wanted to see these bars filled up, they particularly motivated me to make more payments and deposits toward both amounts (and forgo unnecessary expenses).

WHAT YOU'LL NEED

* Journal, one blank two-page spread
* Pencil and eraser
* Ruler
* Black fine line pen, 0.05 mm
* Stickers or washi tape
* Colored brush pen

WHAT YOU'LL DO

1 Create a header at the top of the left page using the black pen.

2 To create the outline for the spreadsheet on the left page, draw a rectangle beneath the header using the black pen and ruler. Leave some space between the header and the top edge of your rectangle and between the edges of the rectangle and the edges of your page.

3 Divide the spreadsheet into four columns. With your black pen and ruler, draw three straight vertical lines inside your triangle. In my spread, the second column is about twice as large as the other three columns.

4 Add labels to the top of each column. You can use the labels that I used for my spread or make up your own.

5 On the opposite page, draw two narrow rectangles near the center of the page. The left rectangle is for my savings tracker. The right rectangle is for my debt tracker.

6 Give each tracker a baseline. For the savings columns, draw the baseline at the bottom of the column. For the debt tracker, draw the baseline at the top of the column.

7 Label each column and add axis marks. Each tracker can have its own scale, or you can draw both columns using the same scale.

8 Use stickers and washi tape to soften the look of the layout.

9 As you start saving and paying off your debt, write down your deposits and payments on the spreadsheet on the left page. Use the brush pen to color in the corresponding amounts in the columns on the right page to track your progress. Fill in the savings tracker starting from the bottom and the debt tracker starting from the top. If you like, you can also start add your goals on the left and right sides of both columns.

MAKE IT YOUR OWN!

This layout can help you achieve any goal that can be measured quantitatively. For example, if you run a website and want to grow your following across multiple social media accounts, you can track your follower or engagement counts in the spreadsheet and create a progress bar for each account.

↠•→ TIP ←•↞

You can split up your goals and transactions into individual trackers for more precise record-keeping. For example, if you are tracking income from multiple sources (e.g., your job, a side business, a blog, etc.), you can create a spreadsheet and savings tracker for each income source and assign it a color.

Datum / Date:

SAVINGS

date	account / notes
11/05/17	sm: repay period opens
11/11/16	sav: direct deposit
11/25/16	sav: direct deposit
12/05/16	sm: monthly payment
12/09/16	sav: direct deposit
12/23/16	sav: direct deposit
01/05/17	sm: monthly payment
01/06/17	sav: direct deposit
01/20/17	sav: direct deposit
02/02/17	sm: monthly payment
02/03/17	sav: direct deposit
02/10/17	sav: bonus check d.d
02/11/17	sm: bonus check!
02/17/17	sav: direct deposit
03/02/17	sm: monthly payment
03/03/17	sm: direct deposit

I use the four columns of the spreadsheet to track the date of the transaction, the account that I'm paying into and any extra notes about the transaction, the amount of that payment, and the balance remaining in the account.

To save space, I use abbreviations for my various accounts. For example, *SAV* stands for my savings account and *SM* stands for my student loans account.

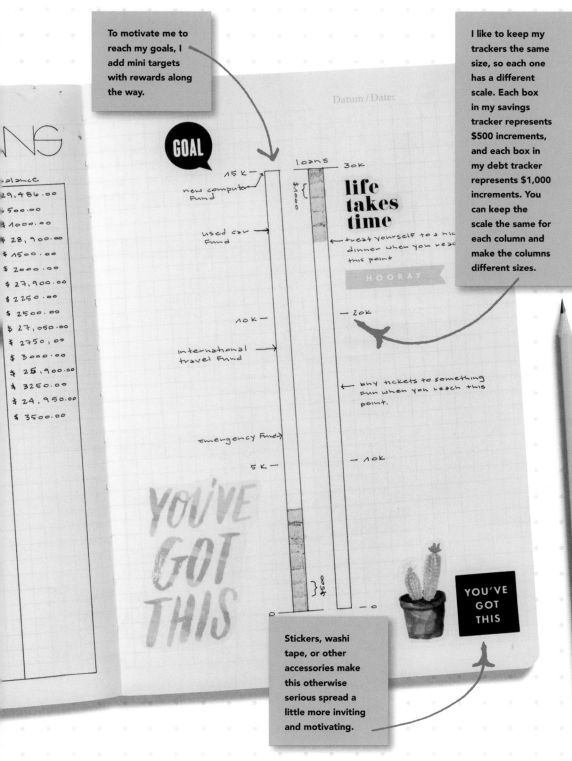

Datum / Date:

To motivate me to reach my goals, I add mini targets with rewards along the way.

I like to keep my trackers the same size, so each one has a different scale. Each box in my savings tracker represents $500 increments, and each box in my debt tracker represents $1,000 increments. You can keep the scale the same for each column and make the columns different sizes.

Stickers, washi tape, or other accessories make this otherwise serious spread a little more inviting and motivating.

GOAL

NS

balance
29,486.00
$ 500.00
$ 1000.00
$ 28,900.00
$ 1500.00
$ 2000.00
$ 27,900.00
$ 2250.00
$ 2500.00
$ 27,050.00
$ 2750.00
$ 3000.00
$ 25,900.00
$ 3250.00
$ 24,950.00
$ 3500.00

15 K —
new computer fund
used car fund
10 K —
international travel fund
emergency fund
5 K —
0

loans   30K
$1000

life takes time

treat yourself to a nice dinner when you reach this point

HOORAY

— 20K

buy tickets to something fun when you reach this point.

— 10K

$500
— 0

YOU'VE GOT THIS

YOU'VE GOT THIS

budget
FOR
september

BILL DUE DATE

M	T	W	T	F	S	S
				1	2	3
4	5	6	7	8	9	10
11	12	13	14	15	16	17
18	19	20	21	22	23	24
25	26	27	28	29	30	

Bills

BILL	AMOUNT	DUE	AUTO	PAID
Rent	1400	9/1		X
Internet	50	9/6		X
Phones	170	9/10	X	X
Credit Card	55	9/14	X	X
Ad Payment	10	9/21	X	X
Car Payment	435	9/21		X
Utilities	55	9/26		X
Insurance	250	9/28	X	
TOTAL:	2,425			

Expenses

Expenses	Budget	Actually Spent
Groceries	500	475
Fuel	150	
Eating Out	200	
Clothes	100	
Entertainment	100	
Emergency Fund	250	
TOTAL:	1300	

Income

Amount	Source	Date
$1,060	MV	9/5
$570	AMA	9/1
$700	Bar	9/8
$1,200	Tips	
$2,400	Chris	9/1

Total Bills + Expenses

$3,725

Left Over

$2,205

4

Monthly Budget Layout

BY ERIN NICHOLS

Keep track of your income and monthly expenses with this easy-to-manage monthly budget layout. With a bill-due-date tracker and space to record your bills, expenses, and income, it's easy to see a snapshot of your finances in one place. Start filling out this spread at the beginning of each month with all of your bills, planned expenses, income, and budgets. Then, at the end of the month, write down what you've actually spent and see how much you have left over.

WHAT YOU'LL NEED

* Journal, one blank page
* Pencil and eraser
* Ruler
* Black fine line pen
* Light-colored marker
* Light-colored highlighter

WHAT YOU'LL DO

1 In the upper left corner of the page, create your header.

2 Next to the header, draw a mini calendar for the month with your ruler and black pen, adding abbreviations for the days of the week along the top. Color the top row that has the abbreviations with your light-colored marker. Use your highlighter to mark the days when your bills are due.

3 Below the header and mini calendar, use your ruler and pencil to create a medium-size box that spans the width of the page and takes up one-third of the space remaining on the page. Add the label *Bills* above the box.

4 Inside the box, draw a horizontal line that spans the whole box near the bottom edge. Write *Total* on the left side of the square in pen.

5 Divide the top section of the box into five columns by drawing four vertical lines with your pencil and ruler. The first column should be wide enough to fit a description of your bills, while the remaining columns on the right side can be narrower. When you're happy with the size of the box and the columns, trace over your pencil lines with black pen and erase any remaining pencil marks with your eraser.

6 At the top of each column, add the following labels with the black pen from left to right: *Bill*, *Amount*, *Due*, *Auto*, and *Paid*. With the marker, color in the row with the labels.

7 Below the box you just created, use the ruler and pencil to draw another similarly sized box and label it *Expenses*.

8 As you did in Step 5, draw a horizontal line near the bottom of the box with the pencil and ruler and write *Total* in pen.

9 Divide the entire box into three columns by drawing two vertical lines with your pen and ruler. When you're happy with the size of the box and the columns, trace over your pencil lines with black pen and erase any remaining pencil marks with your eraser. Label the columns with the black pen from left to right: *Expenses*, *Budget*, and *Actually Spent*. With the marker, color in the row with the labels.

10 In the remaining space below the expenses box, use the pencil and ruler to create a smaller box that spans half the width of the page. Label it *Income*.

11 Divide the box into three columns. When you're happy with the size of the columns, trace over your pencil lines with black pen and erase any remaining pencil marks with your eraser. Label them with the pen from left to right: *Amount*, *Source*, and *Date*. With the marker, color in the row with the labels.

12 To the right of the income box, write *Total Bills + Expenses*. Draw a line below the words. Leave a space between the words and the line to fill in a number later.

13 Below the line, write *Left Over*. Draw a second line below these words. Leave a space between the words and the line here as well.

14 To use the Bills table, fill in the columns with the names of your monthly bills, the amounts due, the due dates of the payments, whether they're paid automatically, and if they've been paid.

15 For the Expenses table, fill in the columns with your major monthly expenses, such as groceries, fuel, and entertainment. Set your budget for each of those expenses in the Budget column. At the end of the month write down how much you actually spent on each of the expenses in the rightmost column in the table.

16 For the Income table, fill in the first column with the amount of income you received, the second column with where it came from, and the third column with the date you received the funds.

17 To calculate the Total Bills and Expenses number at the end of the month, add up all of the numbers in the Amounts column of the Bills table and the Actually Spent column in the Expenses table. To calculate the amount you have left over at the end of the month, add up all the amounts in the Income table and subtract the number written beneath Total Bills and Expenses from this total.

Spending Tracker

BY EMMA BRYCE

Create this simple monthly spending log to keep track of your purchases. By tracking your expenses here, you will see at a glance how much you have spent in the month. This is particularly useful if you are using a credit card as you don't want a nasty surprise when the bill arrives. I also find that if I have to record my spending, I question myself and ask, "Do I really need this?" It's a way of keeping my spending under control!

WHAT YOU'LL NEED

* Journal, one blank two-page spread
* Pencil and eraser
* Ruler
* Circle stencil or compass
* Fine line drawing pens in various widths
* Colored pencils and pens

WHAT YOU'LL DO

1 At the top of your left page, write your header with a fine line pen and decorate it, if you like.

2 Decide and color-code the categories that you want to track. For example, you can consider bills, food, gas, entertainment, and so on. Write out the categories underneath the header and fill in a square of color next to each one.

3 Create the table for recording expenses. Below your color-coding legend, use a pencil to mark the corners of the box that you use for your table. Draw the edges of the box with the fine line pen and ruler, using the pencil marks as a guide. Be careful not to smudge the ink!

4 To create the columns of the table, draw three vertical lines with a ruler and fine line pen. Make one wide column on the left for a description of the items and expenses, a narrow one next to it for color coding, and then two medium-size ones for recording the price and your remaining budget. Label the columns. I usually leave out the name of the color-coding column because it is so narrow.

5 Repeat Steps 3 and 4 to draw another table on the right page. You can continue drawing more boxes on as many pages as you need. For a month's worth of tracking, I recommend four pages. If you have a lot of expenses and need more room, feel free to add extra pages!

6 After shopping, write down all your purchases in the first column of the table. In the two columns on the right, put the price of each item and then calculate how much of your budget remains. To color-code your purchases, fill in the space in the second column from the left with the colored pencil that matches the category.

»•→ **TIP** ←•«

Use any extra space in the legend to write down the total budget for each category for easy reference.

The color-coded legend outlines all the colors that you've used for each category.

Record what you have bought and instantly see how much of that month's budget you have left.

$Spenc$

Groceries
Water
Electric
Other bil
Mortgage

Item / Expen

Grocery Shop
Cinema Ticket
Water Bill
Dinner date
Mortgage
Electric bill
fuel
Birthday prese
Phone bill
New coat
New hat

12

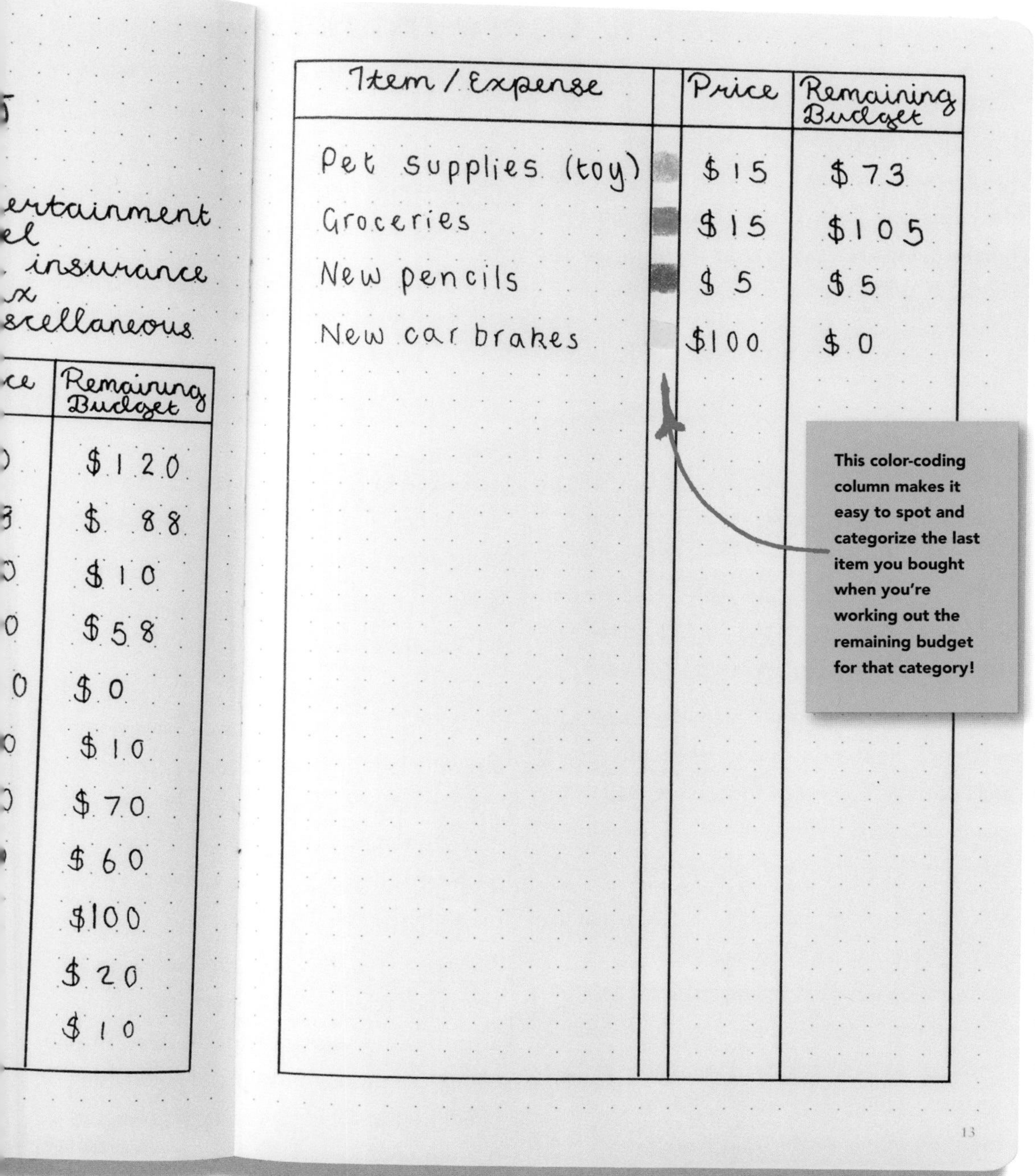

Item / Expense		Price	Remaining Budget
Pet supplies (toy)	▩	$15	$73
Groceries	▩	$15	$105
New pencils	▩	$5	$5
New car brakes	▩	$100	$0

This color-coding column makes it easy to spot and categorize the last item you bought when you're working out the remaining budget for that category!

Left page (partially visible):

...5

...ertainment
...el
...insurance
...x
...cellaneous

...ce	Remaining Budget
	$120
	$88
	$10
	$58
	$0
	$10
	$70
	$60
	$100
	$20
	$10

Monthly Chore Tracker

BY EMMA BRYCE

Use the tracker to see which roommate or family member does the most chores! With this design, you don't have to turn your journal horizontally, so it is very user friendly and aesthetically pleasing.

WHAT YOU'LL NEED

* Journal, one blank page
* Pencil and eraser
* Ruler
* Fine line drawing pens in various widths
* Colored pencils

WHAT YOU'LL DO

1 Draw the banner. Using your pencil, sketch a rectangle, then the ends of the ribbon. Once you're happy with the result, use a fine line pen and ruler to outline it. Write the title of the page inside the banner, and add color, if desired.

2 Draw a double-headed arrow beneath your header. Write the dates of your month above and below it. The dates for the first half of the month should go above the arrow, while the dates for the second half should go below it.

3 With a pencil and ruler, draw a box beneath the numbered arrow. Draw two vertical lines inside the box to create three columns. Make sure that the middle column is as wide as the arrow. For the right column, the number of people in your household will determine its width. You should outline one box for each

person. Draw horizontal lines to create a row for each chore. Each row should be tall enough to contain two smaller rows of squares.

4 Fill in all your chores in the spaces of the left column.

5 Split each space of the right column in half crosswise. Split the bottom cell again into individual entries, one for each person. Put the first letter of each household member's name in the top section. Assign a color to each person and fill in the initialed square in the right column.

6 When someone completes a task, use the assigned pencil color to draw and fill in a corresponding square for that day. At the end of the month, fill in the total number of colored squares for each person in the column on the right.

March Daily Chores

List your chores in the first column of the table.

← 1 2 3 4 5 6 7 8 9 10 11 12 13 14 15 16
17 18 19 20 21 22 23 24 25 26 27 28 29 30 31

The squares correspond to the days of the month, as numbered above and below the arrow at the top of the page.

Chore		Tally
Laundry		P 12
Ironing		P 16
Cooking Dinner		P 8
Set the table		P
Feeding Pets		P 6 / A 3 / E 9 / A 8
Dishes		P 9 / A 5 / E 4 / A 13
Put away Laundry		P 12 / A 3 / E 11 / A 2
Tidy downstairs		P 5 / A 0 / E 7 / A 7
Tidy bedrooms		P 6 / A 3 / E 4 / A 8
Clean Bathroom		P 2 / A 2 / E 3 / A 3
Garbage out		P 4 / A 0 / E 0 / A 0
Clean out Animals		P 0 / A 4 / E 0 / A 0
Recycling		P 0 / A 0 / E 0 / A 4
Clean Kitchen		P 0 / A 0 / E 6 / A 0
Gardening		P 3 / A 2 / E 4 / A 6 / P 0 / A 4 / E 0 / A 0

Track who has completed each task the most.

Cleaning

M

☐ MAKE BED

☐ WASH DISHES

☐ LAUNDRY

☐ DUST

T

☐ LAUNDRY: SHEETS

☐ MAKE BED

☐ VACUUM

☐ MOP FLOORS

W

☐ MAKE BED

☐ WASH DISHES

☐ SCRUB BATHROOMS

☐ SWEEP PORCH

T

☐ MAKE BE

☐ WASH DIS

☐ WIPE AP

☐ CLEAN O

CLEANING SUPPLIES

✓ MICROFIBER CLOTHS

✓ DUSTING SPRAY

✓ GLASS CLEANER

✓ MULTIPUROSE CLEANER

✓ VACUUM

✓ FLOOR STEAM CLEANER

BIG
WEE
CHO

151

Weekly Cleaning Spread

BY MICAH LEWIS

Ever since I created a cleaning routine in my journal, our home life has been totally different. Don't get me wrong . . . I was cleaning lots (and lots) already. But now that it's all scheduled, it's much easier to keep our home clean and calm all the time. Knowing what needs to be done each day simplifies my life, and writing each task down means there is less for my brain to worry about. Whether you enjoy cleaning or not, a schedule like this can really help save the day. Who knows? You might start to *enjoy* cleaning if you get to check off so many boxes.

WHAT YOU'LL NEED

* Journal, one blank two-page spread
* Pencil and eraser
* Large circle stencil or compass
* Black fine line drawing pens, in different widths
* Colored pencils
* Fine point colored markers

KE BED   ☑ MAKE BED

SH DISHES   ☑ WASH DISHES

EEP KITCHEN   ☐ DUST LIGHTS

KITCHEN   ☑ BIG WEEKLY CHORE

◯ WIPE BASEBOARDS

◐ PURGE CLOSET

◯ WASH WINDOWS

This is a rotating task list for larger cleaning projects. Whatever you don't complete this week can be added to next week's Big Weekly Chore list.

WHAT YOU'LL DO

1 Using a pen and a circle stencil or compass, draw three circles horizontally across the center of the left page. Draw three additional circles across the center of the right page. Each circle corresponds to each day of the week that you clean. You can add or remove circles, depending on your routine.

2 Draw smaller circles inside each circle to create a border. If you color-code your days of the week in the other spreads of your journal, you can use the same colors for your circles to match the other spreads in your journal.

3 Write a block letter inside each circle to represent the day of the week. Color the space around each letter with a color of your choice. (Black was used in this example.)

4 Beneath each circle, list the cleaning tasks to be completed that day and draw checkboxes next to each task. Leave some space at the bottom of each page for your *Cleaning Supplies* and *Big Weekly Chore* lists.

5 On the bottom of the left page, create your cleaning supply list. List the items that you need to complete your tasks. Draw circles instead of checkboxes next to each item to help this list stand out from your list of cleaning tasks.

6 On the bottom of the right page, create a *Big Weekly Chore* list. Based on how motivated you're feeling, you can pick which big project to knock out. Any tasks that you don't complete can be moved to next week's list.

7 Near the top of both pages, draw a header across that reads *Cleaning Routine*. Underneath your header, draw fun little doodles representing the cleaning tasks to be completed each day. Use colored pencils and fine point markers to add fun color and shadows to your doodles.

8 Each day, fill in the respective boxes as you get those cleaning tasks completed. Doesn't your house look nice and sparkly?

MAKE IT YOUR OWN!

* This spread can easily be compressed into one page by turning your journal page horizontal and drawing smaller circles.

* You can expand this cleaning spread to cover your entire year! Each circle can represent a different time frame (e.g., daily, weekly, bimonthly, monthly, biannual, and annual), with the corresponding cleaning projects that need to get done listed underneath. Now you're a cleaning rock star!

* You can also easily use this layout as a weekly to-do spread. List out your daily tasks—instead of cleaning tasks—underneath each circle.

Reusable Meal Planner

BY EMMA BRYCE

When I first started my journal, I knew I wanted an efficient way to meal-plan that was reusable. After a bit of trial and error and lots of inspiration from others, the method here is what I came up with. It made meal planning and food shopping easier by providing inspiration on the left hand page and space to write down the ingredients on the right. If your plans change, it's easy to move the flags around, and you can even save them in the back of your journal to reuse another time, especially if you have some foods that are in your regular rotation.

WHAT YOU'LL NEED

* Journal, one blank two-page spread
* Pencil and eraser
* Ruler
* Fine line drawing pens in various widths
* Paper sticky-page flags
* Sticky notepad

WHAT YOU'LL DO

1 At the top of your left page, write out your *What's for Dinner?* header.

2 Think about the meals you cook regularly and divide the meals into categories based on their main ingredient. You will assign each category a different colored sticky-page flag.

3 To create the table on the left page, draw a box beneath your header with a fine line pen and ruler. Divide the box in half lengthwise to make two columns. If you prefer, you can sketch in pencil first and then outline it in ink. Remember to erase the pencil marks once the ink is dry.

4 For your first category, stick a page flag in the assigned color at the top of the left column and label it with a fine line pen. Below the flag, fill in all the meals in that category. Repeat for the remaining categories. Outline the box with a fine line pen, if desired.

5 On the right side of the right page, affix a page from your sticky notepad. Write *Shopping List* in pen above it.

6 On the top of the right page, write *Meal Plan* with a pen and the days of the week down the left side of the page. Leave enough space to place a sticky page flag between each day.

7 When planning your meals for the week, place a flag labeled with your chosen meal and in the assigned color under the corresponding day of the week. Then write all the ingredients needed on the shopping list. You can pull off the list and take it with you to the store.

»»•→ **TIP** ←•«

You can create three separate meal planners in your journal, one each for breakfast, lunch, and dinner.

MAKE IT YOUR OWN!

There are lots of ways you could adapt this reusable spread. For students, try swapping out the ingredient categories with ones that cover extracurricular activities, assignments, and classes. You could also outline a medicine-taking schedule, gym plans for the week, or even a daily planner. To create a reusable daily planning page, use flags to write down any recurring tasks and change the days of the week on the right page to times of day.

When you are stuck for ideas for dinner, take a look at this idea page for inspiration.

WHAT'S FOR D

Chicken

Roast Chicken
Chicken tray bake
Enchiladas
Fajitas
Chicken Pie
Mustard Chicken
Chicken curry

Pork

Roast Pork
Sausages - and mash
— Casserole
— toad in hole
Pork Chops

Beef

Roast Beef
Chilli con carne
Steak and Chips
Steak Pie

48

Meal Plan

monday →
Leftovers

tuesday →
Sausage & Mash

wednesday →
Carbonara

thursday →
Salmon fillets

friday →
Chilli

saturday →
Leftovers

sunday →
Roast Chicken

shopping list

- Bread
- Milk ☐
- Butter ☐
- Sausages ☐
- Potatoes ☐
- Eggs ☐
- Spaghetti ☐
- Cheese ☐
- Salmon ☐
- Green Beans ☐
- Broccoli ☐
- Mince ☐
- chillies ☐
- chopped toms ☐
- Chicken ☐
- Stuffing ☐
- Gravy ☐
- carrots ☐
- pudding ☐

A larger sticky note from a notepad gives you room to write your shopping list. Once you are finished, you can peel off the list and take it with you to the supermarket.

Use sticky flags to write out what you want to eat for the week. If your plan changes, you can move the flags around as needed.

49

R?

crepe
trout

ato
Bacon

training
my ne

goals

List the goals or tasks that you would like to accomplish as a pet owner.

- house training completed
- learned sit & down
- practiced walking on a leash

timeline

```
W1  →  bring her home ●
    →  start house training ○
       ● take out every hour
          when not crated

W2  →  start teaching sit ○
    →  check in on house
       training ●
       - aim for < 2 accidents
         per day
    →  walks ≥5x/week ●

W3     practice sit ●
    →  teaching down ●

W4  →  goal check in ○ ● ●
```

This is your personal overview for how you would like your goals or tasks to progress.

2

py month
1

do

ment complex + register
ership

apartment

names + where to
om

the stuff listed below.
ed!

buy

• bed
ay   • crate / blanket
          • brush
ag   • nail clippers
          • puppy
             shampoo

3

The right side of
the page helps you
prepare to adopt
an animal or list
items that you
need on a regular
basis such as food
or toys.

HOUSEHOLD ROUTINES

Pet Owner's Planning Spread

BY ASHLYN MUESER

I originally created this layout to help a puppy parent prepare to adopt and train a new pet. Even if you don't have a new canine companion, you can adapt this spread to welcome and care for any animal into your home, whether it is a cat or a bird.

WHAT YOU'LL NEED

* Journal, one blank two-page spread
* Pencil and eraser
* Ruler
* Black fine line drawing pens, 0.5 mm, 0.3 mm, and 0.1 mm
* Black brush pen
* Colored markers

WHAT YOU'LL DO

1 Using the pencil, sketch in the header on the top of the spread.

2 With the pencil and a ruler, draw two boxes on each page. The width of each box should span each page. The length of each box will depend on how much room you want for each section. In my example, I made the Goals box smaller, while the Need to Do and Need to Buy boxes each take up half a page.

3 Label each box with the 0.3 mm fine line black pen. Write the labels at the top edge of the boxes. You can add doodles at the corners of the boxes, if you like.

4 Outline the edges of the boxes with the 0.3 mm pen, leaving any parts touching the doodles or labels in pencil. Use the black brush pen to outline the header. After the ink dries, erase any pencil marks.

5 Fill in the Goals section with things that you want to do with your pet. Draw open circles next to each entry that you can fill in when the task is completed.

6 To use the Timeline section, draw a narrow rectangle in the left side the box. Divide the rectangle into equal sections. The number of sections will depend on how many days, weeks, or months that it will take to accomplish your goals. Label each section with your chosen unit of time and add color to the sections with your markers. Draw arrows pointing outward from the time line and write down the amount of progress that you want to make by this point. Add a circle next to your description. This circle will be filled in once you completed this goal.

7 Fill in the Need to Do, and Need to Buy sections with goals or shopping items, using the 0.3 mm fine line black pen. Draw open circles next to each item.

8 Once you purchase an item or complete a goal, use the colored markers to fill in the open circles.

⇶•→ TIP ←•⇷

If you're using this spread to prepare to bring home a new pet, be sure to create and fill in this layout before bringing your new friend home. You'll be quite busy when your animal companion arrives!

MAKE IT YOUR OWN!

While certain aspects of the spread, like the training time line, may not apply for all animals, you can replace such sections with a space to write down notes for vet's appointments or as a growth tracker. I found the Need to Buy section incredibly helpful while preparing to bring home my puppy, Kuna.

Daily Diary Spread

BY CRISTINA TAMAS

Writing a few sentences at the end of each day will not only give you the opportunity to unwind and reflect upon your day, but also it preserves great memories. This page provides you with space for journaling a few sentences each day, and including it in your monthly setup will be a reminder to do it every day.

WHAT YOU'LL NEED

* Journal, one to two blank two-page spreads
* Black fine line drawing pen or any pen of your choice
* Colored markers and pencils (optional)
* Stickers (optional)
* Washi tape (optional)

WHAT YOU'LL DO

1 Start by writing the name of the month at the top of the left page. You can decorate your header, if you like.

2 At the left margins of the pages, write down the days of the month. The number of lines you allocate for each day is completely up to you. Experiment with the amount of space you allocate for each day and adjust it in later diary spreads according to your needs. Separate each day with a long dash.

3 Decorate the pages with doodles, stickers, or washi tape.

4 Use the space you allocated to write a few sentences about what happened each day, similar to what you'd write in a diary.

»•→ TIP ←•«

If you need more inspiration or ideas on what you could write, try choosing some prompts for each day. This will give you the opportunity to reflect on topics that wouldn't otherwise occur to you.

MAKE IT YOUR OWN!

You can use this spread to paste some pictures that you took that month to keep as memories. If you need more space for the pictures, feel free to skip the drawings or adjust the space that you allocate for each day. It will be a trial-and-error process to find out how much space you'll usually need, but about four lines for each day is a good starting point.

august

1 — Tim & I had a lovely roadtrip this wee
to go visit his parents. it's always so g
exactly what I needed to recharge my ba

2 — Hectic day @ work. Tasks keep piling up
office - probably because the deadline is
the presentation tomorrow. I hope a nice

3 — I can't believe the presentation got pus
that by this time today I'd be stress
things as they come, but something ab

4 — So the presentation went much better t
I was so worried about! The project w
with a really delicious lunch. Ugh, a we

5 — I had such a good day today! I fell as
and I woke up at 7am! That's M ho
grocery shopping after work and ma

6 — Fridays have got to be my favorite d
of course! Had a pretty chill day at
and we all surprised her with a cake

7 — Got a bunch of housework done today
barely noticed how much I had negl
now it looks brand new! I'm exhaus
absolutely nothing tomorrow. I nee

48

8	
9	
10	
11	
12	
13	
14	
15	
16	
17	

So I kept my promise and did absolutely nothing but relax all day! I'd forgotten what that feels like... I better not get used to it! ☺ I cuddled up on the couch and watched a bunch of movies til late at night.

Mondays... Why must you be so cruel?! I stayed up late and woke up with a huge headache. No amount of coffee could ever replace a good night's sleep. Met up with Sarah after work. She dyed her hair and it suits her so well! Uneventful day @ work. Had some time to look for ideas on how to redecorate my room - gotta save up some more though, before I can get started on it. Watched a movie and went to bed early this time.

Tiring day @ work + a bunch of errands = me exhausted! I was thinking of going to the gym again but I don't know where I'd be able to fit this into my schedule. Maybe I'm just looking for excuses...

Spent the whole day @ the office today and got a bunch of things done. Being productive always puts me in such a good mood! Sarah told me that she needs a workout buddy, which is such a coincidence! We're starting next week.

or 12 hours
ere, so it's
eek to come.
tension in the
ervous about
with the stress.
had hoped
ow to take
always gets me!
t know what
e celebrated
off my shoulders!
st night at 8pm
sleep. Went
ner - yumm!
ght after Saturday
aura's birthday
with Tim @ lunch.
week that I
ne car too, and
mined to do

Reflecting about your day in a few sentences is a very approachable way to record valuable memories that will bring you joy in the years to come.

If you want, use any extra space at the bottom of the page to express your creativity with doodles or simply add stickers or washi tape.

Dividing the page into smaller sections ahead of time makes the spread less intimidating to fill out daily.

SEPTEMBER
daily positivity

F	1	Octavia slept through the night.
S	2	Had a great workout!
S	3	Got 3 solid hours of writing. Very productive.
M	4	Chris made dinner.
T	5	Had a pumpkin spice latte
W	6	Hung out with my sister.
T	7	Down 2 pounds from last week!!
F	8	Worked on some skill building activities
S	9	Washed and folded all laundry before work.
S	10	Made great tips!
M	11	
T	12	
W	13	
T	14	
F	15	
S	16	
S	17	
M	18	
T	19	
W	20	
T	21	
F	22	
S	23	
S	24	
M	25	
T	26	
W	27	
T	28	
F	29	
S	30	

There is enough space on each line for a short sentence about a positive event or moment in your day.

These horizontal lines make the spread look cleaner and separate each day from the others.

3

Positivity Diary

BY ERIN NICHOLS

Bring more mindfulness into your life and recognize that there is something positive in each and every day with this simple-to-set-up spread. Use this layout to record a positive event or moment every day, no matter how big or small.

WHAT YOU'LL NEED

* Journal, one blank page
* Pencil and eraser
* Ruler
* Black fine line drawing pen
* Double-ended highlighter in a pastel color

WHAT YOU'LL DO

1 Start by making a medium-size header at the top of your page. To create the same header in this example, use the thicker tip of your pastel highlighter to write the month in large letters. Outline the letters using the fine tip of the highlighter. Below the month, write *Daily Positivity* with your black pen.

2 Below the header, sketch a rectangle with your ruler and pencil. Make sure your rectangle can accommodate the all the entries and that it will provide space for a full line of writing for each daily entry.

3 When you're happy with the size of the rectangle, use your ruler and your black pen to ink the pencil outlines.

4 Along the left side of your page, draw another vertical line inside the rectangle to create a column for the days of the week and the dates.

5 In the left column, write the days of the month and the first letter of the corresponding day of the week. In my spread, I wrote the day of the week before the dates, but feel free to write the date first if this works better for you.

6 Use the highlighter to color in the left column.

7 Finally, with your ruler and the fine tip of your highlighter, draw horizontal lines to separate each daily entry. When all the ink is dry, erase the pencil marks.

8 Fill in this spread in the evening by spending a few minutes thinking about your day. Keep your entries short to avoid running out of room.

MAKE IT YOUR OWN!

You can also use this spread as a gratitude diary. Just change the header!

Gratitude Diary

BY MICAH LEWIS

It's the little things in life that mean the most, and journaling provides a way to reflect on all those wonderful small moments. When you take time to record the good in your life, the bad seems to magically diminish. Having a gratitude page in your journal to track what you're thankful for will have a positive impact on your daily outlook.

WHAT YOU'LL NEED

* Journal, one blank page
* Pencil and eraser
* Ruler
* Small circle stencil, $\frac{5}{16}$ inch (8 mm) in diameter
* Black fine line drawing pen, any width
* Colored pencils
* Fine point colored markers

WHAT YOU'LL DO

1 With your pen, start by creating a beautiful *Daily Gratitude* header at the top of the page. Draw something that makes your heart go pitter-patter.

2 Using a pencil and ruler, draw three long rectangles that span the length of the page beneath the header. Divide each rectangle into evenly-size boxes for each day of the month. An extra box can be placed above the middle column beneath your header if your month has thirty-one days.

3 Draw a vertical line inside each of the three long rectangles, near the left edge to create a margin for each entry.

4 Using your stencil and pen, draw a centered circle on the left edge of each box for the dates. You can also draw your circles free hand. Don't worry about imperfections—they help make your journal more beautiful! Label each circle with the day of the month.

5 With your pen, outline the edges of each box, leaving any lines intersecting the circle labels in pencil. When the ink dries, erase any leftover pencil marks.

6 Color in each margin to make the boxes pop off the page.

7 Return to this spread every day to fill in the boxes with events for which you are grateful. They will add up quickly!

Daily Gratitude

1	BEAUTIFUL VIEWS! HEALTHY BREAKFAST. THOUGHTFUL HUSBAND.	**11**	WONDERFUL GIRL TALK WITH A DEAR FRIEND. SHARED PIE!	**21**	MY FAVORITE TREAT IN THE PARKS. FUN GIRL CHATS IN LINE.
2	MAKING UP SLEEP. DONATING FOR OTHERS TO USE!	**12**	NEW COOKIE RECIPES. AWESOME TURN-OUT FOR HELPING JULIE.	**22**	FLOSSING PAID OFF! NO CAVITIES! TIME TO DECOMPRESS.
3	SWEET LESSON AT CHURCH, REMINDING ME OF MY WORTH.	**13**	FOR WINDOW SEAT TO SEATTLE! FUDGE AT MY FAVORITE SHOP.	**23**	AWESOME PHOTOS BY KAREN! FUN NEW PROFILE PICTURE
4	SUCH A GREAT CROWD FOR RICK'S SURPRISE PARTY!	**14**	HEALTHY SALAD FOR LUNCH, & LOTS OF EXPLORING ON-FOOT.	**24**	
5	LOTS OF LITTLE ERRANDS GETTING DONE. RELIABLE CAR.	**15**	DOING NERDY TOURIST THINGS. HOT CHOCOLATE AT SEATAC. BIG HUGS.	**25**	
6	ME DAY! TIME FOR MYSELF, TO ASSESS MY GOALS & BREATHE.	**16**	NEW VACUUM IS INCREDIBLE! SWEET FAMILY TIME AT PARK.	**26**	
7	SEEING IMPROVING MUSCLE TONE! NICE CAMPING GEAR.	**17**	GREAT LESSON FROM BISHOP ON HUMILITY. SWEET CUDDLE TIME.	**27**	
8	GORGEOUS SCENERY ON DRIVE. GOT OUR FAVORITE CAMP SITE!	**18**	GETTING TO THE GYM EVEN THOUGH BED DIDN'T WANT ME GONE.	**28**	
9	RAIN-PROOF TENT REALLY IS RAIN-PROOF. FIRE-COOKED MEALS.	**19**	GIRL TIME IN MY HAPPY PLACE! SHORT LINES & NO CROWDS!	**29**	
10	SAFE DRIVE HOME. WILDFLOWERS FROM RICK & KYLE! SWEET!	**20**	SOFT BEDS & GOOD SHOES FOR ACHING FEET. LOTS OF WALKING.	**30**	

Label each box with the date so you can easily find all the happy things taking place.

It doesn't take much—even a few simple words can help you remember the best parts of your day.

Memory Lane Layout

BY MARIETHERES VIEHLER

I love to add a Memory Lane spread to the first pages of my journal. It helps me remember the most beautiful moments of the year and cherish them forever. I add a gratitude list to the bottom of each page as well. Here, I write the three things I'm most grateful for each month—narrowing the list makes each one even more special.

WHAT YOU'LL NEED

* Journal, three blank two-page spreads
* Pencil and eraser
* Ruler
* Black gel pen
* Circle stencil or a round object
* Colored brush pen (optional)
* Stickers (optional)

WHAT YOU'LL DO

1 With your pen, create a header on the left page. You can include the months each spread will cover, if you like.

2 With your pencil and ruler, draw a horizontal line across the two-page spread.

3 With your pencil, trace the circle stencil or a round object to make two circles on top of the horizontal line running across each page. You will use one circle for each month.

4 To create enough pages to cover a whole year, repeat Steps 1–3 on the remaining two-page spreads.

5 With your pen, write down the names of the month inside the corresponding circles. You can also use stickers, if you like.

6 Outline the circles and the parts of the horizontal line that connect the circles in ink.

7 To create the gratitude lists, write down the numbers 1, 2, and 3 under each circle with your pen. HIghlight the numbers with a brush pen, or just use stickers instead.

8 Erase all the extra pencil marks. Make sure to let the ink on the page dry first!

9 Write down your memories and draw a line to connect them to the month they happened.

MAKE IT YOUR OWN!

You can customize the layout for a specific topic. For example, record favorite moments from a special trip by changing the months into days, or create separate spreads for school or family member.

memory lane

100K
followers

Road Trip
scandinavia

○ **september** ○

○ **october** ○

○ **november** ○

○ **december** ○

mallorca

1st Journal
workshop

Each memory can be a story or just one word. You're only limited by the space in your notebook.

1. internet community
2. Being able to work from home
3. Business opportunities

1. Maxs constant support
2. internet friends
3. Being self-employed

1. My customers
2. Being able to live in London
3.

1.
2.
3.

Gratitude lists for each month are nice add-ons. They make you appreciate the big and little things in your life.

⇻●→ TIP ←●⇺

Adding illustrations, photos, or mementos is a fun way to decorate the spread. You can do this with washi tape or glue.

Memory Gallery

BY MICAH LEWIS

You can create a gallery of your month by sketching little doodles showcasing your best memories. This page is one of my favorites because it evokes lots of happy feelings. Smiling burns calories!

WHAT YOU'LL NEED

* Journal, one blank page
* Pencil and eraser
* Ruler
* Black fine line drawing pens, in different widths
* Colored pencils
* Colored fine point markers

WHAT YOU'LL DO

1 At the top of the page, draw a beautiful header with your pen.

2 With your pencil, draw boxes all over your page, leaving a small section of the page blank. The boxes don't have to line up neatly—be creative with your layout! Once you've finished, draw smaller boxes inside larger ones to create drawings of instant film prints. Ink the pencil lines when you're ready.

3 Draw curved lines with your pen to represent the clothesline from which to hang your "photos." Draw clothespins to attach your photos to the clothesline.

4 As wonderful moments occur throughout the month, draw doodles that capture the highlights you want to remember and write captions inside each frame. Don't let your artistic abilities prevent you from trying the memory gallery! Even stick figures can capture a happy memory in your journal.

5 In the extra space at the bottom of the page, label the section *Favorite Quotes.* Use this part of the page to record snippets from your favorite conversations.

6 Add color to each doodle with colored pencils and markers.

MAKE IT YOUR OWN!

You can simplify this spread by eliminating the clothesline and clothespins. Just draw doodles throughout a blank page to capture your sweet memories.

June MEMORIES

Don't forget to label the month! A quick glance tells you which one you're recording.

Seattle — JUNE 13 –15

Rick's Birthday!

The sky's the limit when it comes to illustrations to show your fun memories.

Camping — 8TH – 10TH

Vacation — 19TH 21ST

FAVORITE Quote: "WHAT'S YOUR FAVORITE ANCIENT REPTILE SEA CREATURE?" –KYLE

This space is a great place to capture sweet sayings you hear from your friends and family.

136

Wish and Gift Lists

BY EMMA BRYCE

Have you seen something you like but can't afford yet? Pop it into your wish list! This helps you stay in control of your spending and serves as a reminder to save up for the things you want. You can also use a variation of the wish list table to create a gift list as well. When someone mentions something he or she would like, just jot down the information here. You'll have holiday and birthday presents sorted out in no time!

WHAT YOU'LL NEED

* Journal, one blank two-page spread
* Pencil and eraser
* Ruler
* Fine line pens in various widths
* Colored pencils and pens

WHAT YOU'LL DO

1 On the left page, use the pencil to mark the corners and roughly sketch the columns of the Wish List table. You should have one wide column on the left and two narrower columns on the right. Once you're happy with the sketch, use a fine line pen and a ruler to draw the edges of the table.

2 Label your columns. The labels of the Wish List columns, from left to right, are *Item*, *Price*, and a checkmark symbol.

3 On the Wish List, draw a second pencil line on the left side of the table and extend it past the top of the table. Using that line, draw a dandelion. Sketch a circle to the right of the line first. Draw the bud of the dandelion near the end of the line and then the seeds from the center of the bud to the edge of the circle. Outline the drawing in pen, wait for the ink to dry, and then gently erase all pencil marks. Color in the illustration.

4 Using the pen, write *Wish List* at the top of the page in cursive. Draw dandelion seeds around the words.

5 On the right page, use the pencil to mark the corners and roughly sketch the columns of the Gifts to Give table. Using the pen, write *Gifts to Give* in cursive. The middle column should be the widest with the two narrower columns on the left and right. Once you're happy with the sketch, use a fine line pen and a ruler to draw the edges of the table. Then draw and color a simple gift in a corner of the page.

6 Label your columns for the Gifts to Give table; the labels, from left to right, are *Who* (for the name of the gift recipient), *Item/Shop*, and *Price*.

7 You're done! Fill in the pages every time you see something you like or have an idea for a gift. Check off or highlight each item after you have bought it. If you have large handwriting, leave an empty row between each item so it is easier to read.

»—•—→ **TIP** ←—•—«

You don't have to keep these pages next to each other. In fact, you might want to keep the gift page in a secret place at the back of your journal!

Wish List

Item	Price	✓
Coloring pencils	$20	✓
Mortarboard charm	$7	
fountain Pen	$20	✓

Fill in the name of the item here and here.

Check off the items once you have bought them, or cross them off if you no longer want them.

Gifts to Give

Who	Item / Shop	Price
Dad	Socks, box set	$30
Mum	New perfume	$50
Amanda	Makeup brushes	$20
Lisa	Scented candle	$30
Phil	Board game	$20
Laura	Gym bottle	$15
Jessica	Recipe book	$10

Write who the gift idea is for—make sure they don't see it!

Fill in these boxes when you finish watching an episode.

Series TRACKER

LOST
I ♡ JACK

Downton Abbey
I ♡ MATTHEW

Movies TO SEE

MARY POPPINS
HIDDEN FIGURES
BAMBI
FIDDLER ON THE ROOF
MOANA
YOU'VE GOT MAIL
HOT SHOTS
NAPOLEON DYNAMITE
INDIANA JONES
AIRPLANE
MEDICINE MAN

Finishing a movie now comes with an extra reward: coloring something in your journal!

Tracker

THE BLUE CASTLE

THE HOBBIT

UNBROKEN

HARRY POTTER #5

HARRY POTTER #6

HARRY POTTER #7

Make your spread
even more personal
by drawing the
plants, lamps, and
accessories that
you have at home.

TV Series, Movie, and Book Trackers

BY MICAH LEWIS

Reading books and having movie and television marathons are important in life. In fact, they may very well be important enough to record in your journal for all the world to see. This spread is a fun way to keep tabs on your current reading list and the shows and movies that you've watched. These pages are also the perfect place to draw some doodles. From camera reels to popcorn kernels to bookshelves, this spread will not only be useful but also beautiful.

WHAT YOU'LL NEED

* Journal, one blank two-page spread
* Pencil and eraser
* Ruler
* Circle stencil
* Black fine line drawing pens, in different widths
* Colored pencils
* Colored fine point markers

WHAT YOU'LL DO

Draw the TV Series Tracker

1 Do some preplanning to research the number of seasons and episodes for the TV shows that you want to track.

2 Measure the amount of space you'll need for each show and its season and episode boxes. Use a pencil to sketch lightly where you want items placed. This will save you a headache later and lets you make sure all of your tables fit just right before you make them permanent with ink. If you're using dot-grid paper, each square on the grid pattern can correspond to one episode. For blank pages, you can create a grid using your ruler and pencil.

3 With a ruler and pen, draw out the boxes for each episode and season. Use the pencil lines that you've sketched as a guide.

> **»•→ TIP ←•«**
>
> When making lines using a ruler and pen, carefully lift your ruler directly upward from the paper instead of pushing it sideways, to prevent smearing the wet ink (unless you like that artsy look of smeared lines).

4 With a pencil (or pen, if you're feeling confident), draw a television in any empty space on your page. In this example, I had room at the top left corner of the page. If you used pencil, trace over the drawing with pen when you're happy with how it looks. Erase any pencil lines still visible after the ink dries With your pen, write *Series Tracker* on the television screen.

5 Label the boxes with the names of your show and the corresponding season and episode numbers. Color in each box when you finish watching an episode.

> **»•→ TIP ←•«**
>
> Drawing alternating lines inside each box instead of filling in a solid block of color creates a pretty pattern as you fill your spread. You could also use little dots, an *X*, or a checkmark to show that you've conquered that episode.

Draw the Movie Tracker

6 To create your Movie Tracker, draw a movie camera with a pencil or pen. With your pen, write *Movies to See* inside the outlines of the camera. You can draw your TV Series Tracker and Movie Tracker on the same page like I've done here, or you can place them on separate pages.

7 Draw popcorn kernels next to and below the camera.

8 With colored pencils and fine-tip markers, color your drawings to really make them come to life! This is your chance to show off all that you learned in elementary school art class. Grab the popcorn, because now you're ready to have a marathon!

9 As you watch a movie, fill in the popcorn kernel with the color of your choice and the name of the film. If everything is filled in, it's probably time to go outside.

Draw the Book Tracker
10 On the right page, write your *Book Tracker* title in pen.

11 Using a pen and circle stencil, draw two circles to make a clock on the left side of the page. Write numbers representing times on the clock and hands showing the time.

12 Draw two bookshelves with your ruler and pen. Draw the spines of the books. Feel free to position them vertically or horizontally.

13 In pen, draw a lamp and potted plant on your shelves among the books.

14 Use colored pencils and markers to color your page.

15 When you finish a book, color in the spine and write the title and date inside.

MAKE IT YOUR OWN!
This spread can be catered to any personal hobby that matters to you. How about a board game or a podcast tracker? Simply update your doodles to match what you're tracking, and you're ready to go!

STEP-BY-STEP DOODLES

BY MICAH LEWIS

Doodles can add so much fun to your journal and make each page a happy space! Even if you don't consider yourself an artist, these tips can help you master simple drawings that you can add to your pages. In the photo in the next page, there are also step-by-step tutorials for the doodles found in my spreads throughout the book so that you can create the same in your journal!

FINDING TOOLS AND MATERIALS:

* For drawing supplies, the higher the quality, the better. Cheaper materials can create unwanted blotches and slight color variations in your journal.
* You can find affordable supplies in surprising places! I often discover wonderful notebooks and writing supplies for about one-third the cost online. Sometimes, they are hidden on shelves in discount department stores. Keep an eye out to find treasures when you're doing your normal shopping.
* You don't have to spend lots of money to get high-quality materials. Watch for fun clearance sales and coupons at craft and art supply stores to get the right pens and pencils for you.
* Around the start of a new school year, large warehouse stores often carry wonderful school and art supplies. Look for amazing deals on colored pencils that will last years!

DOODLING TRICKS AND TIPS:

* The Internet is there for a reason. Search for simple pictures, and then sketch your own versions until you're satisfied enough to add them to your spreads.
* If you're worried that your first doodling attempts won't be journal-worthy, practice on a separate piece of paper until you can give yourself a high-five.
* Beginning in pencil can always reduce frustration later. Draw out potential doodles in erasable lead, and then draw over the lines in ink when you're happy with the results.
* When you're picking colors, think about how different colors make you feel, and then find ways to incorporate your favorites into your journal. I like bright, fun, happy colors and prefer cool colors to warm ones.

* When adding shading, I usually darken the right side of the shape and add more layers of color as I move downward in an arc. You can use the same color but press a little harder to add dimension. Try to imagine your light source; then darken the side opposite to it.

* It can be so frustrating for your pens and markers to bleed through a page. Always test your pens in a discreet place. I use a pen test page in the back of my notebook, so no blank pages are damaged.

* Use thick paper to prevent bleeding or "ghosting" of your ink. Paper is measured in different weights—the higher the number, the thicker the paper. To be able to use every page in my journal without ink ruining the day, I use paper that is at least 70 lbs. (100 gsm) or higher.

* Smudges are never a happy accident. Depending on your pen, you might need to let a page dry before placing another page on top. Blowing softly to help the ink dry faster usually works wonders. I hate to say it, but sometimes patience is best! Go make a hot chocolate for yourself while the ink dries.

Project Planning Page

BY CRISTINA TAMAS

If you're working on a personal project, this spread will help you organize and visualize every step with spaces for your goals, budget, time line, and sketches or inspirational pictures. It's especially useful for long-term craft or design projects.

WHAT YOU'LL NEED

* Journal, one blank page or one blank two-page spread

* Black fine line drawing pen or any pen of your choice

* Colored markers, highlighters, and pencils

WHAT YOU'LL DO

1 Start by writing the name of the project at the top of the page with a pen.

2 With your pencil, divide the remaining space into as many sections as you need to organize the project. I usually include the following sections: *Purpose/Goals*, *Budget*, *Shopping List*, and *Timeline*. Make sure to dedicate a space for sketches or inspiring pictures. The size of this space will depend on your project and how much room you need for your images. Don't worry about fitting everything on one page. This layout will evolve organically as the project progresses.

3 Write your headings in with a fine line black drawing pen, allow the ink to dry, and erase any remaining pencil marks. Then use colored highlighters so that to your headings stand out.

4 To use this page, just start filling in your lists in the sections. Add an open circle or square so that you can check off items as you finish them, especially in the Purpose/Goals and Shopping List sections. Draw sketches and place pictures in the space you made in Step 2.

TIPS

* For more elaborate projects, feel free to use an additional page to add more sections or write down a more detailed overview of all the stages and deadlines of your project.
* You can use an empty page to create a mood board for inspiration and attach samples of materials or clippings from magazines.

bedroom makeover

Write down what you want to accomplish to stay focused and motivated.

[PURPOSE/GOALS]

- O DONATE OLD / UNUSED ITEMS
- O LESS CLUTTER - MORE SPACE
- O PAINT THE WALLS
- O MODERN / MINIMALISTIC DECOR

[BUDGET]

- O FURNITURE : $1500
- O DECOR : $600
- O MISCELLANEOUS : $300

[SHOPPING LIST]

- O BOXES FOR DONATING ITEMS
- O PLANTS: 3 SMALL ; 1 LARGE
- O NEW DESK + DRAWER CABINET
- O NEW DESK CHAIR
- O FOLDERS FOR DOCUMENTS
- O COATHANGERS
- O NEW CURTAINS + MATCHIN
- O 2 LAMPS + NEW LIGHTING FI
- O DRESSER
- O 3-4 PAINTINGS / WALL DEC

Use this section to write down the project's main stages.

[TIMELINE]

- M: PREP ROOM FOR PAINTING
- T: PAINT ROOM
- W: DONATE / SELL ITEMS
- T: SHOP FURNITURE
- F: SHOP SUPPLIES / DECOR
- S: ASSEMBLE FURNITURE
- S: DECORATE + CLEAN

[DECOR VIBE]

- O MODERN / MINIMALISTIC
- O SOFT / PASTEL COLORS
- O WALLS: OFF-WHITE
- O COLORS: WHITE + GREY
- O ACCENT COLORS: TEAL, BLUE, GREEN

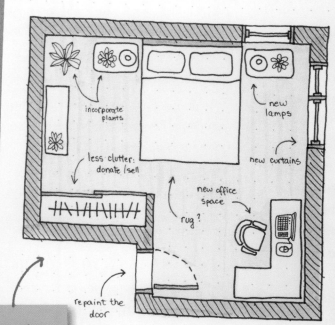

incorporate plants

less clutter: donate / sell

new lamps

new curtains

new office space

rug ?

repaint the door

Draw or paste pictures to help you visualize the goals of the project.

Feel free to add any sections that are specific to your own project.

Travel Itinerary Layout

BY CINDY THOMPSON

Sometimes planning for a trip is just as exciting as actually traveling. Since I usually don't have time to journal on a daily basis when I'm traveling, I like to have a solid plan in place, along with a few extra options in case I have more time than expected or if something falls through. To help keep my plans organized, I like to use one page in my journal to track everything in one place.

WHAT YOU'LL NEED

* Journal, one blank page
* Ruler
* Black extra fine line pen, 0.5 mm
* Colored brush pen
* Stickers or washi tape

WHAT YOU'LL DO

1 Create a header at the top of the page. In my spread, I used black pen to write *Travel* and a brush pen to letter *Maui*.

2 On the right side of the page below the header, draw a narrow rectangle the length of the page using the black ink pen and ruler. Label the rectangle *Packing List*.

3 Draw another rectangle in the bottom left corner of the page using the black pen and ruler. This rectangle should fill the space between the left edge of the page and the Packing List. Add the label *Notes* at the top of the box using black pen.

4 Draw a line at the top of the page using black pen. The line should be aligned with the top of the Packing List box.

5 Write down the first travel date above the line. You can use your brush marker to highlight the day to add color. List any important preplanned events with their start times or reservations in the space below the line.

6 Repeat Steps 4 and 5 for your other travel days. Leave a space between each entry.

7 Fill in the Packing List with your travel essentials. Leave a free space next to each entry for check marks.

8 Add any additional travel notes or adventure options to the Notes box.

9 Decorate the page with stickers or washi tape.

MAKE IT YOUR OWN!

For longer adventures, you can spread the layout over multiple pages. For each additional page, add the itinerary and Notes sections, but leave out the Packing List. Without it, the itinerary and notes can now span the width of the page.

Datum / Date:

TRAVEL *maui* HI

day 1 - 1 july 2017
- 9a - Flight departs pdx [gate c22]
- 12p - arrive at OGG, pick up rental car
- 4p - check in at resort
- 7p - dinner

day 2 - 2 july 2017
- visit banyan tree and tour lahaina
- shop at Foodland for poke
- 6p - dinner

day 3 - 3 july 2017
- swimming w. kids before lunch
- 2p - parasailing [ka'anapali beach wlk]
- meet family for bbq dinner at resort

day 4 - 4 july 2017
- snorkling [honolua bay]
- pick up snorkle gear from bass frogs op:8a
- 6p - dinner

day 5 - 5 july 2017
- check out of resort by 10a
- 2p - Flight departs OGG

notes
- shopping at whaler's village
- jet skis @resort (don't need to reserve)
- Iao valley state park for hiking
- maui ocean center (aquarium)

packing list
- ✓ identification
- ✓ wallet/cash
- ✓ tickets
- ✓ glasses
- ✓ sunglasses
- ✓ tissues
- ✓ first aid
- ✓ medication
- ✓ tooth brush/paste
- ✓ skincare
- ✓ haircare
- ✓ makeup
- ✓ brush
-   heat tools
- ✓ outfits +1
- ✓ underwear +2
- ✓ socks +1
-   jacket
- ✓ swimwear
- ✓ shoes
- ✓ accessories
- ✓ cellphone + ch.
- ✓ tablet + ch.
- ✓ headphones
- ✓ camera +ch
- ✓ battery pack
-   journal
-   pen case
-   printer
- ✓ memory cards
- ✓ water bottle
-   pillow

packing list

Looking for a specific item on the list is a lot easier when everything is divided into sections.

clothing

- ☐ ☐ Underwear
- ☐ ☐ Socks / Tights
- ☐ ☐ Bras
- ☐ ☐ Sleepwear
- ☐ ☐ T-Shirts
- ☐ ☐ Dress Shirts
- ☐ ☐ Jeans / Pants
- ☐ ☐ Shorts
- ☐ ☐ Dresses
- ☐ ☐ Shirts
- ☐ ☐ Sweaters
- ☐ ☐ Coat / Jacket
- ☐ ☐ Cardigan
- ☐ ☐ Sneakers
- ☐ ☐ Sandals
- ☐ ☐ Dress Shoes
- ☐ ☐ Boots
- ☐ ☐ Snow Boots
- ☐ ☐ Hiking Shoes
- ☐ ☐ Laundry Bag

The two check-boxes make sure that you pack all the essentials before you leave for your trip and that you won't forget them on your way back home either

Accessories

- ☐ ☐ Hats
- ☐ ☐ Gloves
- ☐ ☐ Scarves
- ☐ ☐ Belts
- ☐ ☐ Jewelry
- ☐ ☐ Purses
- ☐ ☐ Swimsuits
- ☐ ☐ Sunglasses

Toiletries

- ☐ ☐ Toothbrush
- ☐ ☐ Toothpaste
- ☐ ☐ Dental Floss
- ☐ ☐ Deodorant
- ☐ ☐ Shampoo
- ☐ ☐ Conditioner
- ☐ ☐ Body Wash
- ☐ ☐ Body lotion
- ☐ ☐ Brush / Comb

- ☐ ☐ Hairspray
- ☐ ☐ Face cle
- ☐ ☐ Face Lot
- ☐ ☐ Sunscree
- ☐ ☐ Contact
- ☐ ☐ Contact
- ☐ ☐ Shaving
- ☐ ☐ Make up
- ☐ ☐ Make up
- ☐ ☐ Tampor
- ☐ ☐ Birth c
- ☐ ☐ Nail Fil
- ☐ ☐ Tweeze
- ☐ ☐ Supple
- ☐ ☐ Medic

import

- ☐ ☐ Boa
- ☐ ☐ Wall
- ☐ ☐ Stic
- ☐ ☐
- ☐ ☐
- ☐ ☐
- ☐ ☐
- ☐ ☐

Miscellaneous

- ☐ ☐ Mobile Phone
- ☐ ☐ Laptop / Tablet
- ☐ ☐ Chargers
- ☐ ☐ Adaptor
- ☐ ☐ Books
- ☐ ☐ Earbuds / Headphones
- ☐ ☐ Ear Plugs / Eye Mask
- ☐ ☐ Tissues
- ☐ ☐ Lip Balm
- ☐ ☐ Camera
- ☐ ☐ Passport
- ☐ ☐ Pencil Case
- ☐ ☐ Journal

The customizable Important section lets you add notes for different kinds of trips or items that are not included in your generic packing list.

Reusable Packing List

BY MARIETHERES VIEHLER

Before I go on a trip, I always make a packing list. I used to make a new packing list each time I went away, but it became very time-consuming to write the same things over and over again. Instead, I now write a very generic list that covers all of my basic necessities and can be reused for any trip I go on. I also add a section where I can write down special things to pack or remember to do for a specific trip. Just make sure to use a pencil to check off the boxes and write down your notes.

WHAT YOU'LL NEED

* Journal, one blank two-page spread.
* Pencil and eraser
* Ruler
* Black gel pen
* Colored brush pen
* Stickers (optional)

WHAT YOU'LL DO

1 Create a simple header that reads *Packing List*.

2 With your pencil, divide each page in half vertically to create guides for your two-column lists. On the right page, draw a horizontal line in the bottom third of the page to reserve space for your Important section.

3 Starting in the right column, create the label for the first section below the header. Begin writing down the items in that section, leaving space at the front of each entry in your list so you can add checkboxes later. Continue your list across the spread, making new sections as needed, until you have written down everything you need. When you reach the bottom of the right column, continue your list on the top of the left column, using the vertical pencil lines to keep your list aligned. As you move onto the right page, make sure your list does not go past the horizontal line.

4 Use a colored brush pen to highlight the different categories, like toiletries or clothing.

5 Draw two squares in front of each item on the packing list.

6 With your pencil and ruler, draw a box in the space below the horizontal line on the right page. Use a pen or sticker to label the box *Important*. With your pen, outline the edge of the box.

7 Draw two checkboxes in front of each item on the packing list.

8 Erase all the extra pencil marks. Make sure to let the ink on the page dry to avoid any smudging.

9 To use the Packing List, check off the first square when you've packed an item. Check the second square when you repack everything for your return home. Remember to use pencil and make light checkmarks so that they are easy to erase later on.

10 To fill in the customizable section, use a pencil to write down what you need for the upcoming trip that's not included in the generic list.

MAKE IT YOUR OWN!

You can easily transform this spread into a reusable grocery list. Use the sections for categories such as produce, meat, dairy, snacks, and more. The space at the bottom of the right page can be used for things you wouldn't usually buy or only need once in a while. Just make sure to use a pencil on these pages too.

Practice Pages

RESOURCES

You can find most of your supplies at any brick-and-mortar craft store or office-supply store, but there are also a variety of specialty retailers that carry a wide range of stationery, writing utensils, and supplies.

* Michaels (michaels.com)
* A.C. Moore (acmoore.com)
* Hobby Lobby (hobbylobby.com)
* PaperSource (papersource.com)
* MochiThings (mochithings.com)
* Muji (muji.us)

Many individual designers also sell stickers, printable templates, and customized stencils on their websites or through their online stores.

Emma Bryce

Emma studied illustration at the University of Gloucestershire and graduated in 2016. While she was a student she started a journal to organize her home, studies, and working life. She started posting different illustrated daily headers and templates on Instagram (@that_journal) and on her website (thatjournal.com). Her favorite things to use in her journal are colored pencils and fine line pens. She likes to read, but she also loves to draw and illustrate—plants and flowers are her favorite things to doodle. She also likes trying out new crafts, such as paper-crafting and crocheting. She lives in the West Midlands in the UK with her parents, sister, two cats, a rabbit, and a flock of chickens. Keeping a journal helps her to keep track of everything!

Micah Lewis

Micah is a huge fan of creative journaling and has seen her life change since 2016 as a result of journaling daily. She works as a corporate jet pilot and flies multiple trips each year to Disneyland. In her spare time, Micah loves to read, play board games with family and friends, design journaling stickers for her online shop, host parties, bake irrational amounts of cupcakes, travel, nest, and spend time snuggling with her cute husband, Rick, and sweet son, Kyle. Micah presently resides with her family near Salt Lake City and flies from Scottsdale, Arizona, for work. She can be found online at myblueskydesign.com and @my_blue_sky_design.

Ashlyn Mueser

Ashlyn is a journaler and designer who loves to use her journal as a creative outlet while organizing her ever-changing life. An engineer by day, she loves to use her technical drawing skills to create layouts and designs to help herself and others plan their lives. She regularly posts on her blog, Blue Nittany (bluenittany.com), and her Instagram (@bluenittany), sharing information on creating designs that work for all types of lifestyles, reviews on various journaling products, and tips on how to start a journal. When she is not journaling, Ashlyn loves to spend time with her puppy, Kuna, and visit family and friends.

Erin Nichols

Erin is an active twenty-something-year-old creative blogger. She lives in Bozeman, Montana, with her fiancé and two young daughters and takes full advantage of the beautiful landscape around her. When she's not at her computer working or doodling in her journal, she's probably walking her dogs, going on a slow and steady jog, or playing in the park with her little girls. You can visit Erin's blog: The Petite Planner (thepetiteplanner.com).

Cristina Tamas

Cristina is a young architect based in London who uses her journal to organize her busy life and release her inner artist. She believes that perfectionism should never stand in the way of creativity, and she's always looking for ways to help others discover a balance between the two. She enjoys quiet evenings spent with family or close friends and is also very active on social media, where she posts pictures of her journal and writes about stationery, planning, and self-improvement. You can follow her @my.life.in.a.bullet or visit her website mylifeinabullet.com.

Cindy Thompson

With a background in engineering and a constant need for a creative outlet, Cindy has always tried to find ways to blend form and function. She started journaling by hand to create a planner that both streamlined her needs and matched her aesthetic, something she couldn't find in any preprinted planner. She quickly realized journaling was a medium with which she could organize with unlimited creativity, and she enjoyed figuring out how to adapt and better her planning ever since putting pen to paper. Cindy currently shares her journaling journey on her blog, plananotherday.com, and on Instagram (@plananotherday).

Marietheres Viehler

Marietheres is a creator from London with a passion for creativity in any form. She has tried many different ways of planning, from a binder planner with preprinted inserts, a traditional calendar, and several smartphone apps. After seeing others upload their first journaling attempts online, she decided to create an Instagram account (@journalspiration) dedicated to everything planning and productivity related. She also opened an Etsy shop called Journalspiration, where she sells her designs for stickers and paper goods.

INDEX